THE GEORGIAN THEATRE OF
RICHMOND, NORTH YORKSHIRE

The front cover shows the restored interior of Richmond Theatre
from the Royal Box, showing the backcloth and wings of 1836.
From a Bowers-Brittain original.
By kind permission of the Georgian Theatre Trustees.

ISBN 0 900657 91 X

Printed in Plantin Typeface
by William Sessions Limited,
The Ebor Press, York, England.

THE GEORGIAN THEATRE OF RICHMOND YORKSHIRE

and its circuit: Beverley, Harrogate, Kendal, Northallerton, Ulverston and Whitby

SYBIL ROSENFELD

The Society for Theatre Research
London

IN ASSOCIATION WITH

William Sessions Ltd., York, England.
1984

Contents

Illustrations

Acknowledgements

WHEN I STARTED TO WORK on the Richmond Theatre I was fortunate enough to meet Miss Lucy Warman and Mr. Edward Bush, both now unhappily dead. Miss Warmam, who was a descendant of Tryphosa Brockell the original manager of the company, allowed me to examine her family papers which included letters and the diary of the Rev. James Tate. They added a personal touch to a chronicle of dates and places, players and plays. Mr. Bush copied the large collection of playbills in the Whitby Museum and generously handed over his results to me. I am sorry indeed that they have not lived to see the book which owes much to them but I would like to dedicate it to their memory.

Many others helped me with playbills or diaries in their possession. Those who kindly allowed me to copy their bills were Mrs. Butler of Milnthorpe, Mrs. Carter of Northallerton and Mr. Ewan Kerr of Kendal, to all of whom I am most grateful. The diary of John Courtney I saw through the kindness of Air Chief Marshall Sir Christopher Courtney. Miss J. M. Bromley, a descendant of the diarist, copied the relevant passages and supplied information.

I am also indebted to *The Westmorland Advertiser* for allowing me to examine their files, and to Mr. J. Dennett, Town Clerk of Beverley who gave me information about the theatres there.

I was greatly encouraged in my work by the late Lady Crathorne and Mr. Donald Brooks, Town Clerk of Richmond, who were chiefly instrumental in having the Theatre reopened.

This was many years ago and more recently I owe much to Mr. Gregor Macgregor who founded the Theatre Museum and to his successor Mr. Brian Rochdale with whose help I discovered new material in the Museum. Mr. L. P. Wenham's articles in the Annual Reports of the Richmond and District Civic Society enabled me to add to my original script. To Mr. Ron Smith and Miss C. A. Pearson of the Barrow-in-Furness Library I owe information about the Soulby playbills which cover Ulverston, Burton, Cartmell and Dalton, and an invaluable list of them.

Without all these my book would hardly have come to life and I offer them my grateful thanks.

I am much indebted to Mr. Ian Herbert for his assistance in editing the book so efficiently, to Dr. Pieter van der Merwe for reading the proofs and to Miss Hilda Schiff for checking the index.

CHAPTER I

The Company's Early Years
1749 – 1788

Although Richmond was only a small circuit town, like hundreds of others, in the theatrical world of the 18th and early 19th centuries, it has for the theatrical historian a unique contribution to make to the annals of the theatre in the English provinces. The uniqueness consists in the fact that by exceeding good fortune, a combination of records exists which cannot be paralleled in any other provincial town in England. In the first place the theatre itself is still standing, and has preserved its main features as a playhouse: and, though it has not, like Bristol, a continuous record of theatrical activity, the changes it has suffered are comparatively few. Also, since the building belonged to the corporation, most of the changes it underwent in the latter half of the 19th century, when it was used for other purposes, may be traced in the Corporation Coucher Books. The history, not only of its alterations and repairs, but also of its lessees is revealed to us from entries recording the corporation's decisions with regard to their property. In the second place there has come down to us a diary and letters belonging to the family which, for several decades, managed the company that acted at Richmond. These were in possession of the late Miss Warman a descendant of that Mrs. Wright who played such a long and important role in the company's life. Lastly an almost complete series of playbills of the company's bi-annual visits to Whitby is preserved there; a number of others are extant over a long period for the annual season at Harrogate; a third set, practically complete, covers the whole circuit for one year from 1st March 1810 to 18th March 1811 and a fourth has recently turned up of 17 handbills for Richmond itself in 1811. These three sources of evidence – the theatre, the family papers and the playbills – enable us to present a fuller and more vivid picture than has hitherto been possible of one of the lesser theatrical companies: of the play house in which they worked, of the lives they led, of the plays they produced and of their methods of production.

The history of the Richmond Theatre cannot be considered by itself but must take its proper place and perspective in an account of the company's activities in other circuit towns; because the actors and actresses were the same, their repertory similar and their methods of presentation would vary but little. What the company played in Whitby in the winter and Harrogate in the summer Richmond doubtless enjoyed in the autumn. But whereas we have few playbills for performances at Richmond itself, the many we have for other circuit towns throw light on the Richmond seasons.

Not very much is known of the theatrical history of Richmond before the opening of the existing theatre in 1788, but Miss Warman's family papers have enabled us to piece together part of the story of the company which played there, since it was managed for many years by members and connections of that family. This history must begin then with the birth at Barnard Castle in 1727, of Tryphosa Brockell, daughter of the Rev. Christopher Brockell, granddaughter of the Rev. William Brockell, and great-granddaughter of the Rev. John Brockell. The first manager of the company, of whom we know anything, was thus descended from a long line of clergymen and from a well known and respected family. Her father died when she was young and she was committed to the care of her grandfather, the Rev. William Brockell. Later on he married his maid, and Tryphosa, turned out in the world, was taken in by a family who also put up as lodgers the theatre folk who visited the town. In this way Tryphosa Brockell met Henry Miller, an actor in a strolling company, and in 1749 at the age of 22, she married him. By this marriage she had two daughters, Jane born in 1750 and Katherine. Both married actors. Jane married Fielding Wallis in 1773 and became in her turn the mother of Tryphosa Jane Wallis (the Miss Wallis of Bath and Covent Garden fame), of Margaret who married the Rev. James Tate, whose diary and letters provide us with such fascinating glimpses of the company and their activities, and of six other children. Katherine, Tryphosa Miller's second daughter, married William Tayleure, the son of a Norfolk clergyman, who had turned to the stage after his father's death.[1] It is a curious fact that both Fielding Wallis and William Tayleure, the two actor sons-in-law of Tryphosa Miller were themselves the sons of clergymen. The company always had a strong reputation for respectability and this must have been enhanced by the family's connections with the church. These were no itinerant vagabonds but educated men and women.

We do not know when Henry Miller died nor when his widow married her second husband, J. Wright. Wright either was or became the manager of the company, and by him Tryphosa had a son, James Brockell Wright, who later became a member of the troupe. After Wright's death, his widow took over the management and, when Fielding Wallis joined the company at Ripon in January 1771, it was she who was running it. Fielding Wallis was born in 1754 and was the son of the Rev. Thomas Wallis, Rector of Boho 1767-94 and of Templecarne 1794-1807 in Co. Fermanagh, Ireland. How he came to be an actor was charmingly related many years afterwards by his daughter, the famous Jane Wallis, in a letter to her sister's children.[2] Here is the story in her own words:

Elizabeth Alexander and I have often conversed upon the strangeness of the conduct pursued towards my *father* the eldest son – sent an apprentice to a bookseller at Dublin – whilst Thomas his junior by many years was educated at the University there. Sent there, my father contracted a passion for the stage – every farthing he scraped together he laid out at the Theatre, where night after night he went – and certainly to something worth seeing. Mossop – Barry – Mrs. Barry – Mrs. Fitzhenry no! that's not the name. Dear! to think I should forget my kind and particular friend's name – with whom on my first going to Bath I became so intimate, and who loved me very dearly. And so – two or three more lads laid their heads together to set off to England and become *Actors*. And here, I must mention another link in the dismal, and yet, let me not call it so, chain of my poor father's fortunes. Old Aunty Peggy – his Aunt – was fond of Shakespeare and used to make my father read it to her. And some passages in some play he got to please her so much that she exclaimed: 'How very well you read that Fielding – read it again.' So he and his cronies scraped money together somehow, got into a coasting vessel and landed at Irvine in Argyleshire, where they went from one station to another, sometimes in want of a bed, sometimes of a dinner, sometimes lying in bed because they had no food to put into their bellies – and all I daresay under assumed names. My father's was Stuart. He lodged once with the Pretender's piper – who thought him so like his dear young King – that he was wont to stand at arm's length while tears rolled down his old cheeks in torrents. Of his – my father's – peregrinations I know [? nothing] till he walked over to Ripon, *I believe* to try for an engagement in Mrs. Wright's (then) strolling company, and there for the first time did he see our dear mother lying with her head upon her arms on a table – pale, dirty, and worn from her long journey, walked to. While her mother, like a second Katherine, sat even there in *Imperial dignity*. Mrs. Tayleure, also married, was her mother's favourite. Whether Mr. Tayleure was already of the company, or joined it afterwards, I do not know, or whether Mr. Butler was then a part of it. But I have often wondered at the strange coincidence of Mrs. Butler (Miss Brockell of an old and respectable clergyman's family) having two daughters, the eldest Jane Miller, married to Fielding Wallis – and her other to Mr. Tayleure also a clergyman's son, and of a most highly respectable Norfolk family – but leave them and let us keep to our own. Till my father was discovered by Mr. Hall (Jack Wharton) he never wrote to his father to say he was living, married and had three children – he then resumed his own name. His father desired the certificate of his marriage might be sent him – he forgave him.

How tenderly it is told: the hardships of the boy of 17 who ran away to be an actor, the romantic story of his meeting with the Pretender's piper and his choice of a stage name, the unforgettable picture of the fine dignity of Mrs. Wright and the utter fatigue of her daughter after their day's tramp. This, our first glimpse of the company might well stand as a symbol of the stroller's life.

Jane Wallis did not know whether Samuel Butler had yet joined the company but two years later he was already married to Mrs. Wright and had taken over the management from her. Born in 1750 he was then only 23, whilst his wife was 46. According to *The Thespian Dictionary* he was in the stay-making business at York and abandoned it for the stage. We first hear of him in a letter from a Mrs. Harrison[3] dated from Guisborough 10th July 1827 in which she sets out to tell what she knows of Fielding Wallis and thus completes for us the story of his reconciliation with his father. Again it cannot be better told than in her own narrative:

About the middle of January 1773 a company of comedians obtained leave of Mr. Chaloner, to perform for a short time in the Toll Booth of Gisbro', a very ancient, and cumberous edifice, and very ill calculated for such a purpose, but the Families of the Dundas's, Halls and Chaloner, being very large, and the danger to Children from such representation, never having at that time occurred, they obtained leave, and considerable patronage, and the Theatre, humble as it was, was very well attended, from all the Villages around, it being I believe the very first amusement of the kind ever exhibited here. –

The Manager, a young man of the name of Butler, had married a Widow of the name of Wright, whose husband had been manager – she had two daughters, both married to Actors in the Company, the one to a Mr. Stuart, the other a Mr. Tayleure, both very lovely young Women, and who maintained the most perfect modesty and decorum, throughout their life of labour and temptation. – Mrs. Tayleure was delivered of a son, a few hours after her return to her lodgings, after acting the very first night of the performance in '*Love in a Village*'. This event caused a particular interest in her favour, and the conduct of both Stuarts and Tayleures, was such, that by the inhabitants of Gisbro' (in the better rank) they were noticed, and invited to their houses.

Amongst others my Father (the Clergyman of the parish) stood forth to countenance and support merit. – It was observed that both off, and on, the stage, Mr. Stuart was absent, and appear'd unhappy; it seem'd singular, that possessing such a Wife, of whom any one might have been vain, there should be a constant cloud upon his brow. – In a

4

short time, he requested of my Father a private interview, and in that, disclosed to him the state of his mind, and a sketch of his history. –

He said he was the son of a respectable clergyman in Ireland of the name of *Wallis*, with no property, but his living, and with a large family. – That he had been put Apprentice to a Stationer at Dublin, but having taken a violent inclination for the Drama, he had quitted business, Family, Friends, and even *Name* and coming to England, had join'd Mrs. Wright's company, where after being a short time, he had married her eldest Daughter. – His filial disobedience had constantly haunted him, and he cou'd bear it no longer, and requested of my father, as the greatest favour he cou'd confer upon him, to be his intercessor and write to his Father in his behalf, begging only for pardon and forgiveness. – My Father wrote directly, saying all Mr. Wallis desired, and adding all, that was true, and just of his Wife. –

In a short time, an answer was return'd, expressing great gratitude for the mediation and passing an act of oblivion over the follies and disobedience of his 'prodigal Son', now so unexpectedly restored to him, giving his blessing to both Son and Daughter, being all he had to give, but that was given freely. – The above named letters, I am grieved to say were not preserved; but I remember well, the tears we shed over Mr. Wallis's and the pleasure we had, in seeing Mr. Wallis Junr recover his spirits. –

Soon after this reconciliation, the Company left Gisbro' and we heard no more of them, and I do not recollect that they visited this place any more.

The respectability and good conduct of the company is stressed by Mrs. Harrison and the interest of the townspeople in the players and their lives and the invitations they received to the houses of the 'better rank' were evidently unusual. Not so remarkable in strolling life, one knows, is the story of Mrs. Tayleure acting until within a few hours of the birth of her child.

A glimpse of the company in 1776 is afforded by Mrs. Wells who became famous for her imitations.[4] As a young girl named Mary Davies she and her mother were given an introduction to Butler by Tate Wilkinson and were engaged by him. His company she says, visited Harrogate, Ripon and Pontefract.

We arrived at a very seasonable time, the company being greatly deficient in dresses, and my mother having brought with her an extensive assortment. The lady who had the management of this company for a number of years married a Mr. Butler, a worthy man, who was at that time younger than her two daughters.

Of Tayleure she says that he was:

A respectable man, and leader of our band. He played first, second, and third fiddle; and though he did not rival Weischel, he justly conceived that a superfluity of instruments would be inconvenient in a small theatre, so that we were never incommoded with any more than he thought proper to play himself.

Mrs. Butler was friendly:

Contrary to the customs of *kings* and *queens* of strolling companies who ever make it a rule to keep their subjects at a great distance, my mother and self were often invited to Mrs. Butler's table.

Unfortunately:

. . . a young lady, a distant relative of hers, coming among us, she was so highly received into favour, that I was for some time kept in the background

this so displeased Mrs. Davies that she took her daughter away to join the Cheltenham company.

In 1774, Tryphosa Jane Wallis, who was to become the well-known Miss Wallis of Bath, had been born to Fielding and Jane Wallis in Richmond, where we may suppose the company was at that time acting.[5] In 1778 Fielding Wallis and his family left the company and returned to Ireland where Fielding was engaged in the Crow Street Theatre in Dublin. At the age of nine in 1783 the little Jane Wallis made her first appearance on the stage at the Smock Alley Theatre as the Fine Lady in *Lethe*.

This same year Butler appeared for one night with the York Company. Tate Wilkinson wrote of him twelve years later:

Mr. Butler is a rival manager. Like the French troops, he seized on my neighbouring territories at Beverley. He is, without compliment, as far as my knowledge can with truth ascertain, or without the least right to doubt, a very honest man, indefatigable in his endeavours, and deserves the esteem and good will with which he is in general supported.[6]

Indeed as a manager he was a strict drill serjeant but through economy and perseverance brought success to the company.[7]

The following year the Wallis family returned to England and rejoined Butler's company. At Pontefract the company played John Lund's *Ducks and Pease; or the Newcastle Rider*, a one act farce which was printed in 1777. The cast list was Wallis, Butler, Mountford, Naylor, Sheridan, Mrs. Wallis. The Wallis's, do not, however, appear in the first playbill[8] we have of the company which is for a performance at Kendal on 21st January 1785. The chief offering on this occasion was the first performance there of O'Keeffe's *Castle of Andalusia* with Butler as Pedrillo and Mrs. Fildew as Catalina:

Mr. Butler flatters himself that the great Applause this Piece has received from the most brilliant and crouded Audiences in London will be sufficient to recommend it to the Ladies and Gentlemen of Kendal, and afford him some Recompence for the great Expence and Trouble he has been at, in procuring an authentic Manuscript Copy, and the Author's Permission to perform it.

The afterpiece was the farce of *The Divorce* and both were given gratis between parts of a concert. Charges were pit 2/-, first gallery 1/-, upper gallery 6d. Nothing under full price was taken and there was no admittance behind the scenes.

Kendal was a new acquisition to Butler's circuit for a playbill of 1783 shows that quite a different company was acting there. The Theatre was the first one in the Woolpack Yard and had been erected in 1776-79.[9]

In the second Kendal playbill[10] for 25th February 1785 Fielding Wallis, his wife and two of his daughters, Jane and Elizabeth[11] figure in a benefit for Mrs. Wallis. On this occasion Hartson's tragedy *The Countess of Salisbury* was performed with the following cast: Longsword – Butler, Grey – Wallis, Morton – Wright, Ardolph – Craneson, Leroches – Smith, Knights – Draycott and Hillyard, Raymond – Williams, Ld. William – Miss E. Wallis, Eleanor – Mrs. Martin, Countess of Salisbury – Mrs. Wallis. The moral effect of the play was duly emphasised on the bill:

> Throughout the whole play it seems to have been the author's design to inculcate this excellent moral, That notwithstanding Providence may for a while suffer the innocent to be oppressed, it nevertheless, in its own good time, snatches them from the arm of violence, and turns their tears to smiles, their anguish to delight.

The tragedy was followed by the famous Hubert-Arthur scene from *King John* played by Wallis and Jane Wallis; and the evening concluded with the first performance of Bate Dudley's comic opera *The Flitch of Bacon* with favourite songs and music as in London. This was cast: Tipple – Butler, Wilson – Craneson, Greville – Draycott, Justice Benbow – Wallis, Ned – Wright, Kilderkin – Hillyard, Patty – Martin, Maj. Benbow – Smith, Eliza – Mrs. Tayleure. A Ms. note at the back of the bill states that £28. 7. 0. was taken and £3 shared. The company was then at this time still on the old sharing basis.

Whilst the company was in Harrogate in the summer the child Jane Wallis appearing on the stage attracted the attention of Lord Loughborough and his wife who soon after adopted her. Then the blow fell and in December 1785 her mother died at Richmond. She had been much loved and was greatly lamented. Fielding was heart-broken and never again would act in Richmond.[12] Two years later he wrote of his feelings and of the adoption of his child by the Loughboroughs to his old friend the Rev.

William Leigh Williamson of Guisborough, through whose mediation he had been reconciled to his father. This letter was copied and passed on by Mrs. Harrison.

Dear Sir,

Tho' the only knowledge you ever had of me, occasion'd you both trouble and expence, yet I presume to write you, on the present occasion, indeed the generous manner in which you then exerted yourself, to serve me, assures me, at least of your forgiveness, and for my request, it is no further made than as it may happen to accord with convenience and propriety. I am also convinced, that you will feel pleasure, in knowing that in the midst of my distresses (the just consequence of my follies) Providence has in some degree made me the instrument of bringing good on that worthy and respectable Man, whose blessing and pardon were obtained for me by you.

Many and various, Sir, have been the changes in my humble fate, since I saw you; a few years afterwards I went to Ireland, where my Father (who was charm'd with my Wife's conduct, as indeed all who knew her ever were) took the three youngest Children we then had, we turned to this country about two years and a half ago, and the following Summer, my eldest child, and her mother, were fortunate enough to attract the notice of Lord and Lady Loughborough, who came to Harrogate, whilst we were performing there in Mr. Butler's company, and after a fortnight or three weeks acquaintance with our Girl, whom they had continually with them during that time, my Lady L. nobly offer'd to take her, and give her the best education possible for two years; this proposal as generous as it was unexpected we gratefully assented to, on which our Benefactress, who was then going on a visit, left a Purse to convey her Charge up to London, where I soon after committed her to their care. – Oh, my dear Sir, I was so happy, I was treated as an equal, and return'd home to Richmond with the strongest assurances, that the most powerful interest would be exerted, to place my Wife at the top of her profession, her merit really was great, and Lord Loughborough gave it as his opinion, that there were only two Actresses in England who cou'd dispute a superiority to her.

Poor thing she was then with Child, and her Friends only waited till she was released from that situation. – She died two hours after the unhappy wretch was born, and left eight of them behind her. – How I loved her God only knows, I have often gazed at her, till tears of rapture ran down my cheeks, while wonder fill'd my heart, that in the way of life she was brought up, anything cou'd be so pure and so innocent.–

The anguish I have suffer'd for her loss, was excessive, and is aggravated by the dreadful certainty, that she might have been sav'd, tho' I had both a physician and Surgeon, to attend her; – that I never can be happy again upon Earth is too true, but I hope the misery I feel is not a sinful one, I am wretched, but I am satisfied. 'Providence orders all things for the best.' If ever virtue left behind it a blessing, my Jenny has bequeathed it to her Children, who are I am told lovely, well disposed, and likely to meet with success in life; – of the helpless group, I have only two on my hands. – My Eldest Girl's amiable manners has establish'd her so much in her angel Benefactresses esteem, that the dear Woman has condescended to declare, 'that she never long'd for life so much, as since their acquaintance' and my Lord told me last York assizes, that he believed my daughter to be everything I would wish; she is treated in every particular as one of their own, and is I fancy highly accomplished. The consequence of all this Sir, you might tremble for, if I did not inform you, that she is supposed to be the greatest Theatrical Genius in the World, and in truth when she left me, she was a prodigy, – but she is not yet quite 14. – In the course of last Spring Lady Loughborough ask'd and obtain'd from her Brother Ld. Courtney a Living he had in his Gift, on his Estate in Ireland, with £160 a year which she directly presented to my Girl, for her Grand Father, who has just got to his own home again, after taking possession of it, for it does not oblige him to relinquish his other Living. –

What satisfaction the event has given me, I am unable to describe, but in spite of all, my mind is tinctured with a melancholy which I fear I can never shake off. –

After plagueing you with this tiresome account of myself, permit me now to mention the more immediate cause of my writing. –

Butler wishes to visit Gisbro' this winter, with his Company, provided he can obtain Mr. Chaloner's leave; he means to wait on him after N. Allerton Races, and in the interim I am free to beg your interest if you can mention the subject to that Gentleman and his Lady. – I dare venture to assert that you can scarcely serve an honester man, and it is but truth to assure you sir, that his Company were by all the Ladies and Gentlemen at Harrogate last year, preferr'd to the York set. – While Butler performs at Richmond (where I never will play, indeed I cou'd not) I propose going up to London, to see my treasure, but if this company visits Gisbro' I shall hope for the honor of paying my respects to you. – I have another inducement for wishing to see that neighbourhood, the satisfaction of waiting on Mr. Hall, whose conduct towards me, at the same time, that it fills my heart with gratitude, proves him to be one of the best and most humane young men in England. –

I am dear Sir your truly obliged and respectful humble servant,

Fielding Wallis!

It is the letter of a man whose sensibility remained undulled by the hard life he had led. Whether his request was granted and whether Butler performed again at Guisborough we do not know; nor can we from such slight evidence of the company's activities establish their circuit; we only know that Kendal, Ripon, Harrogate, Richmond and Northallerton were among the towns visited. Harrogate was apparently shared with the York company who must have visited it at a different season or possibly in alternate years.[13] If Wallis's statement is true, that the inhabitants and visitors preferred Butler's troupe, it is a great testimony to them because the York company under Tate Wilkinson, was at this time one of the best provincial companies and commanded some famous actors and actresses. Butler followed Wilkinson's example of strict punctuality and was rewarded by success and public approbation.[14] There is no doubt that Butler's company was doing well since he was able to open a series of new theatres in the next few years: Harrogate and Richmond in 1788, Kendal in 1789, Ripon in 1792, Northallerton in 1800 and Beverley in 1805. Some impetus to this was probably given by the Act passed in 1788 which legalised dramatic performances in the provinces, and allowed justices to grant licences to strolling companies to act for 60 days at a time, a second licence being obtainable, after eight months' interval, in the same place and, after six months, in the same jurisdiction. Up till that time provincial companies, unless they had been granted a royal patent, were really operating illegally.

We first hear of the new theatre at Richmond in a holograph letter from Butler to the Mayor dated 26th October 1787.[15]

Mr. Butler's respects to the Mayor and Corporation of Richmond and as he wishes to accommodate the Town and Country in a more commodious manner he will with their approval and assistance erect a proper theatre.

There being a place in their possession would suit for that purpose adjoining the Quaker Meeting, he begs leave to make the following proposal.

He will rebuild the place as a Theatre upon Lease for one and thirty or one and twenty years in such a manner that if at any time hereafter, the Lease is not renewed as a Theatre it may be converted into dwelling houses, he will pay the rent it now lets for, or what the Gentlemen of the Corporation think proper.

If agreeable he hopes they will make an order, as he wishes to settle everything for the Building while he is here.

He remains with due respect their much obliged humble servant,

S. Butler.

LAST NIGHT THIS SEASON.

FOR THE BENEFIT OF
MR. & MRS. BUTLER.
THEATRE-ROYAL, RICHMOND.

On FRIDAY Evening, 19th of October, 1810
THEIR MAJESTIES' SERVANTS
Will perform a Favourite NEW DRAMA, (Never Acted here) called THE

Free Knights;
OR THE
EDICT OF CHARLEMAGNE.

Prince Palatine,	Mr. SMITHSON,	Walbourg,	Mr. MARTIN,
The Abbot of Corbey,	Mr. WILSON,	Christopher,	Mr. BUTLER,
Baron Ravensburg,	Mr. DAVIS,	Oliver,	Mr. GEORGE,
Count Roland,	Mr. BENNETT,	Falconer,	Master MEADOWS,
Ravensburg	Mr. JEFFERSON,		
Bernardo,	Mr. HALLAM,	Countess Roland	Mrs. WILSON,
Everard,	Mr. G. BUTLER,	Ulrica,	Mrs. JEFFERSON,
Zastrow,	Mr. DUNNING,	Agnes,	Mrs. BUTLER.

WITH NEW SCENERY, PAINTED BY MR. DUNNING.

A SPACIOUS CAVERN,
With a new set of ROCK WINGS, and BRAZEN DOOR,
where the FREE KNIGHTS kept their Prisoners, and held their Court.

A VIEW OF CORBEY ABBEY. A CHATEAU.
THE GATES OF CORBEY,
A SPLENDID GOTHIC HALL.

THE STATUE OF CHARLEMAGNE.
THE INSIDE OF CORBEY ABBEY,
With Banners of the FREE KNIGHTS, Inscriptions, &c.

A Comic Song, called "THE GREAT BOOBY," by Mr. DAVIS,

To which will be added a FARCE, called

A BEGGAR
ON HORSEBACK.

Old Codger,	Mr. DAVIS,	Goby Barnavag,	Mr. HALLAM,
Horace,	Mr. JEFFERSON,	James,	Master MEADOW,
Cosey,	Mr. GEORGE,		
Corny Buttercup,	Mr. BUTLER,	Mrs. Mummery,	Mrs. MURRAY,
Scout,	Mr. DUNNING,	Nancy Buttercup,	Miss JEFFERSON,
Tweedle,	Mr. SMITHSON,	Mrs. Neighbourly,	Mrs. WILSON,
Barnavag,	Mr. WILSON.	Miss Barnavag,	Mrs. DAVIS.

BOXES, 3s. PIT 2s. GALLERY, 1s.——To begin at seven o'Clock.

Plate I.   Richmond: 19th October, 1810.

MR BUTLER AS CARACTACAS.

MR BUTLER as WALDER the AVENGER.

Plate II.   Samuel W. Butler as Caractacus in
Mason's Caractacus.

Plate III.   Samuel W. Butler as Walder in The Avenger.

(Courtesy the Museum of London.)

His petition was presented on 1st November, and a lease granted to him of the:

> . . . aforesaid Tenement and premises now in the occupation of Mr. Jas. Masterman and his under-tenants, for the term of 21 years from the 12th day of May next at the yearly rent of five pounds clear of all taxes whatsoever which are to be paid by the Lessee on condition that the said S. Butler shall at his own expense, pull down, the present buildings and in the place thereof erect a proper theatre according to some plan and Elevation in the meantime and without delay to be delivered to and approved of by Mr. Alderman Wayne and Mr. Ald. Hickes and Mr. John Readhead and Mr. P. Macfarlane two of the Common Council.

The committee or their agents, besides approving the plan and elevation, were enjoined from time to time:

> . . . to inspect and superintend the Building of such Theatre in order that the same may be erected and completed agreeable to the approved plan and comformable to the said S. Butler's petition.

The Mayor was to give notice to quit to James Masterman in due time.

Unfortunately, no trace has been found of the plan and elevation. Nor does it seem possible to discover where Butler played in Richmond before this new theatre was opened. It was evidently not in the Common Hall since, though there are entries in the Coucher Books for this Hall's letting to William Craggs for Assembly night, there is no mention of the players.

The demolition and the rebuilding took under four months. In the meantime we have our second playbill of the company for a performance of *The School for Scandal* and *The Lyar* at Beverley on 14th May 1788.[16] Beverley had been in the York circuit until 1771 when the Mayor ordered Tate Wilkinson out of the town and he lost 'the little jewel Beverley from the crown of my York imperial diadem'.[17] How soon afterwards Mrs. Wright or Butler took it into their own circuit we do not know. The theatre where they played was in Walkergate.[18]

The charges for admission were 2/6d. for boxes and lattices, 2/-for pit and 1/- for gallery. The performance was for the benefit of Bell, and the other actors were Dalrymple, Day, Sullivan, Stanfield, Snagg, Whyte, Tayleure, Wright, Jones and Fildew. Butler himself played Sir Peter Teazle. For this and most subsequent Beverley seasons up to 1806 we are fortunately enabled to catch a more personal glimpse of the players through entries in the diary of an assiduous local playgoer – John Courtney.[19] It seems to have been the custom at Beverley for a concert to be given for the benefit of one or two of the players and on 28th May Courtney records: 'We were at a Concert for Benefit of Messrs. Wright and Meredith – M. sang five songs, last again without Musick – Charming.' On 16th June we read 'I and my son Henry who came to me after 2nd Act were at the Play. Benefit of Mrs. Jones. *Jealous Wife* and *Midnight Hour*.' They went again on 18th June: 'last night of season. *He Would be a Soldier* and *The Poor Soldier* – Jack came at Half price.'

Whilst his theatre was in the course of construction at Richmond, Butler opened a new one at Harrogate on 1st July 1788. Up till that time the company had played in a barn behind the Granby Hotel. The new theatre was situated in High Harrogate, a short distance east of Christ Church on the Stray.[20] Boxes and green (upper) boxes cost 3/-, pit 2/-, gallery 1/-, and places for the boxes had to be taken at the theatre. On Tuesday, 12th August, a benefit was given for Fielding Wallis,[21] at which Cumberland's comedy *The Fashionable Lover* was followed by Mrs. Inchbald's farce *Appearance is Against Them*. In the comedy Butler played Colin Macleod, Stanfield – Mortimer, Wallis – Aubrey, Mrs. Tayleure – Lucinda Bridgmore; in the farce Butler played Humphrey. Others who took part were Dalrymple, Wright, Day, Henry, Jones, Snagg, Martin, Mrs. Fildew, Mrs. Stanfield, Mrs. Martin, Mrs. Jones, Mrs. Wright and Mast. Tayleure. This must have been the composition of the company when the theatre was opened at Richmond. It was, as was usual with country companies, very much a family affair. Butler himself is said[22] to have been a useful actor without much claim to merit. His best part was Clodpole in *Barnaby Brittle*. He fancied himself in Scottish roles but his accent was Yorkshire. Mrs. Butler may not have acted herself, but, as we have seen, both her daughters by her first marriage, Mrs. Wallis and Mrs. Tayleure, did, and her sons-in-law also. Then there was her son James Brockell Wright by her second marriage and his wife who had been Juliana Hillier. And the next generation was already on the stage in the person of Master William Tayleure who played a servant in *Appearance is Against Them*. Of the others James Field Stanfield was an Irishman and the father of the painter Clarkson Stanfield; he left the company soon after to take a leading part in the Scarborough company.[23]

Canon Tate, writing in 1832, remembers making the acquaintance of Stanfield in Richmond in 1788;[24] he mentions that both Stanfield and Wallis were freemasons and that Stanfield was very fond of the young Jane Wallis, who was still at that time residing with the Loughboroughs. As for Mary Fildew and John Martin they were to prove the company's most faithful members. Mrs. Fildew continued to play almost up to the time of her death in 1815 and Martin did not disappear from the cast lists until 1818. A remarkable record since it was the way of strollers to change companies frequently. This devoted service is indeed a tribute to the company which evoked it.

CHAPTER II

Years of Prosperity
1788 – 1800

THE NEW RICHMOND THEATRE was opened on Tuesday, 2nd September 1788 with a performance of George Colman the Younger's comic opera *Inkle and Yarico* and Mrs. Inchbald's comedy *The Midnight Hour*. Some years later the theatre was described as 'a neat house, well fitted up, and the scenery and other ornaments very appropriate'.[25] And we have the actual building to give us a very good idea of what the theatre looked like on that opening night.

James Tate, then a lad of 17, was present on the occasion and notes in his diary:

The New Theatre opened. A Prologue by Stanfield spoken by Butler. Inkle and Yarico and the midnight hour. Side scenes etc. by Cuit and Coatsworth. The Theatre very elegant. Earl Fitzwilliam, Sir Thos. Dundas, etc. etc.

Both pieces performed were very new, *Inkle and Yarico* having been brought out at the Haymarket Theatre on 4th August 1787 and *The Midnight Hour* at Covent Garden on 5th May 1787. Quite what Canon Tate means by the side scenes remains a mystery. If he was referring to wings why did not the same artists also paint the rest of the scenery? It is possible that back cloths from other plays were used and only the side scenes were fresh, but *Inkle and Yarico*, with its scenes of a forest with a ship at anchor in the bay and of a quay at Barbados with an inn upon it, would seem to call for its own back cloths.

As for the artists, George Cuitt the elder[26] though born at Moulton in 1743 had settled in Richmond. He was then a man of 45 years of age; he had exhibited portraits and landscapes at the Royal Academy and was at that time frequently employed by the neighbouring gentry to execute commissions. Locally he was quite a figure though I have found no other records of his activity as a scene painter. He died on 2nd February 1818.[27] Coatsworth was a local decorator and carpenter, but all the information I have been able to gather about him is a notice of his death in the *York Chronicle* of 13th February 1812: 'Lately, aged 52, Mr. Coatsworth of

Richmond, painter.' Possibly these artists were also responsible for the decorations of the theatre. The only other glimpse of this season at Richmond is contained in a note by James Tate:

> Thursday, Sep. 25th Rood Fair 1788. A riot in the Theatre occasioned by Robert son of the Rev. W. Thistlewaite of Kirby Fleetham, who had inlisted into the Foot Guards but was released next morning by his friends. Fielding Wallis came on to the stage to remonstrate.

The company must have spent the winter in Kendal for in 1789 the old theatre there was deemed too small and a new playhouse was opened in Woolpack Yard. This served as the theatre until 1823 when it was sold to the Scottish Seceders for a chapel. It subsequently became a dancing academy and is now the Christian Science Church.

By 1st April 1789 the company was in Beverley since we have a playbill[28] for this date: 'By Desire of the Gentlemen of the Thursday Night's Club, Theatre Royal, Beverley.' It is interesting to note that the theatre here was dignified by the title of Theatre Royal. Harrogate did not adopt this title until sometime between 1803 and 1806, Whitby not until 1805-6, but by 1810 all the theatres in the circuit were announced as Theatres Royal. No patents, however, seem to have been issued. The play was *The Clandestine Marriage* in which Penson played Lord Ogleby, Butler – Sterling, Mrs. Fildew – Mrs. Heidleberg and Mrs. Tayleure – Miss Sterling. *The Quaker* was the afterpiece with Craneson playing the title role. The Pensons, Thorpe and Cresswell are new names. Penson had started his stage career in Stanton's Stafford circuit in which he had played the low comedy line for a few years. He left them to engage with Butler but stayed with him only a short time as in October 1789 he joined the York company on Tate Wilkinson's invitation. Many years later he rose to an engagement at Drury Lane.[29]

The performance started at 6.30 and 'Tickets and places in the Boxes (were) to be taken at the Theatre each day from Ten till one o'clock'. John Courtney has much to say this season of a Master Weston 'a fine pleasing little boy' who called on him on 4th May with a bill and tickets: 'We liked him so much that we took tickets for us all.' They duly went to the theatre that evening to patronise the benefit of Mr., Mrs. and Master Weston.

> *As You Like It* and *Tom Thumb*. It was only a moderate house and I wished it had been fuller. Miss Weston sang very well indeed and Master Weston acted Tom Thumb very well. We took the little girl into the Front Box to see her brother act Tom Thumb and my wife asked her and her brother to dine with us next Thursday.

They went on 7th June and Courtney is full of their praises:

> The Westons are the finest children I think I ever saw. They are remarkably sensible, lively and entertaining. In afternoon she sang and acted'

14

So taken was Courtney with the young players that he resolved to recommend them at Harrogate. He invited them to dine again the following week:

I came home to Tea, they sang to me. I was quite sorry to leave them as they were to go away next day – poor Things – They were sweet engaging children.

It is a delightful picture and it shows the interest taken by the gentry in the child players who were such an inevitable feature of strolling companies.

It was whilst Butler was at Beverley that he engaged Thomas Dibdin to play with him at Harrogate. Dibdin, sailing from London to Hull took a stage-coach thence and joined the company at Beverley.[30] He has described it for us:

I found the company consisted of the manager; a Mr. Wright, said manager's wife's son; Mrs. Wright, and her sister, Miss Hilliar [whom Dibdin was to marry three years later]; there were also related to the manager a large family of Tayleures: the father played first violin, and Sir George Airy; one of the sons played Dogberry as well as I think I ever saw it acted; another son is now performing at the English Opera; Mrs. Tayleure, Mrs. Fildew, a Mr. Saville, with Mr. and Mrs. Jones, and Mr. Martin, an Irish prompter with one eye, who, when under the influence of the rosy god, would put his quizzing glass up to the eye he had not.

Dibdin boarded both in Beverley and Harrogate with the Jones family and learned the violin from Mr. Jones, for whom he subsequently procured an engagement in the Liverpool Theatre. Mrs. Jones who played the fashionable young ladies, later became a leading actress in the Norwich Theatre.

The company journeyed from Beverley to Harrogate where they had an eventful summer season. Miss Wallis, who was still residing with the Loughboroughs and was then 15 years old, played with the company.

She had already appeared at Covent Garden on 10th January as Sigismunda in *Tancred and Sigismunda* and she seems to have been in the habit, for the next few years, of joining her grandmother's company in the summer months. (She also played Belvidera on 21st January, Rosalind in *As You Like It* for her benefit on 11th February, and Roxalana in *The Sultan* on 19th February.)[31] But a greater than she also deigned to play four nights with them during their sojourn in Harrogate. Dorothy Jordan on her way to Edinburgh had arranged to give a benefit for Tate Wilkinson at Leeds. She got as far as Harrogate:

When a subscription purse from the company at the different hotels so strongly tempted her, that she agreed to recruit herself there for three of four days, and diversify the amusements of the devotees to sulphurated springs.

Though by doing so, she made herself liable to a penalty of £500 for being late for her engagement in Edinburgh.[32] As she finally appeared in Leeds on 8th July, her performances in Harrogate must have been given just prior to this date.

Harriot Mellon, later to become the Duchess of St. Albans, and her mother Mrs. Entwistle, who were staying at Otley, trudged to Harrogate to watch Mrs. Jordan and Miss Wallis play. After the performance was over they were too tired to return to Otley and too poor to hire a lodging, so Miss Hilliar volunteered to put up Harriot Mellon if another actress in the company would take charge of Mrs. Entwistle. As each one in turn excused herself Mrs. Entwistle is said to have sat on the stage throne all night.[33]

That unreliable writer Mrs. Cornwell Baron-Wilson adds that:
> Mrs. Jordan played several of her best characters there supported by the elite of the company, the manager and his wife, T. Dibdin, Miss Hilliar, the Tayleurs, and others of less note.

She also tells a tale that Butler, desirous of showing attention to Lady Loughborough with whom Miss Wallis was staying, put up a singular notice in the Green Room, which Harriot never forgot. 'Notice – The gentlemen of the theatre are requested not to wear their hats while Miss Wallis is in the house.' Of course each actor found some reason why he should wear his, and all in concert acted in direct opposition to what they called 'Butler's stuff.'

Miss Wallis is described[34] as:
> . . . very young, exquisitely fair, with expressive blue eyes; all the movements of her fine figure indicated native grace and elegance, but her voice had more sweetness than strength.

She seems to have been a charming rather than a brilliant actress. Perhaps she played that year in Richmond when the company was there in the autumn, but we have no record of it. By October she was playing in Bath where she was to remain until 1794 when she returned to Covent Garden.

The company may possibly have gone direct from Richmond to Ripon, but there was probably an intervening port of call. 23rd February 1790 was the sixteenth night of the Ripon subscription so that, if they performed three nights a week as was usual, they must have opened in Ripon about the middle of January. A playbill for 23rd February advertises Mrs. Inchbald's *The Child of Nature* for the second time with Mrs. Wright as Amanthis, the Child of Nature, Mrs. Jones as Marchioness Merinda with the epilogue and Farquharson as Marquis Almanza, his first appearance on this stage. This play had only appeared at Covent Garden in November, 1788. It was followed by Allen Ramsay's *The Gentle Shepherd* with Patie – Townsend, Roger – Jones, Gland – Smith, Symon – Wright, Sir William – Warwick, Blandy – Butler, Jenny – Wright, Mause – Mrs. Fildew, Margery –

16

Mrs. Martin, Peggy – Mrs. Tayleure. The site of this theatre is not known, but it was evidently a small and poorly equipped building as no boxes are advertised, only pit 2/-, gallery 1/-. No admittance was permitted behind the scenes and no servants were allowed to enter without payment.

By 25th May 1790, the company was back in Beverley. John Courtney records in his diary that day:

> I was at the Play; Benefit of Mr. Smith and Mrs. Cresswell. *Tender Husband* and *Midnight Hour*.

By June Jane Wallis had rejoined them. She also gave a few performances in York in mid June.[35] There is a further entry in John Courtney's diary under 2nd June 1790:

> I and my wife were at the Play. 1st night of Miss Wallis's Child of Nature – Amanthis by Miss Wallis. I had taken several places for every night she performed and we filled them. She acted amazingly well and was a very pretty girl – I was much entertained.

On 5th June we read:

> At the Play *Tancred and Sigismunda*. Miss Wallis played Sigismunda extremely well, indeed she had the richest dress on I think I ever saw on the Stage; it was given her by Lady Loughborough and cost an Hundred Pounds, it was most brilliant and superb, indeed she looked and performed vastly well. It was the same she had on in London when she first performed there. We did not stay for the Farce.

On 7th June the diarist saw Miss Wallis play Rosalind in *As You Like It* which was followed by *The Agreeable Surprise*:

> Miss Wallis looked vastly well in all her different dresses and played vastly well indeed. The House was very full again.

On 9th June a large party went to her benefit:

> *Conscious Lovers* Indiana by Miss Wallis and the *Sultan* Roxallana by Miss Wallis – It was with great difficulty got the Boys in – I never saw the House so full – Miss Wallis had the whole of what was Recd. tonight without deducting expenses 44 pounds an amazing sum. We sat in Prince's S[tage] box, very hot. Miss Wallis had a most superb Turkish dress made by herself by Mrs. Otley's Directions. Twelve pounds they say was turned away tonight.
>
> When I called on Mr. Wallis in ye morning at — lodgings to get tickets he asked me to go upstairs which I was sorry I did not as I wanted to have seen Miss Wallis off the stage – and to have talked to her about Lady Loughborough &c. He and I talked about her as I was at Harrogate when Lord and Lady L. first saw her – I told him my wife would hope to see Miss Wallis if she should be longer in Town.

How proud Fielding Wallis must have been of his young daughter who was everywhere winning admiration, packing the theatre and fulfilling the promise of her talent as an actress. New actors were Sandford, Dunn, Bailie, Nelson and Holbrook, actresses were Mrs. Sandford and Mrs. Kay.

Jane Wallis also acted for two nights with the company in Harrogate this year. On 26th June she played Amanthis in *The Child of Nature* which was followed by *The Waterman*.[36] On 1st July she played Sigismunda (and spoke the epilogue) to the Tancred of Saville. She was sufficient draw even at this early age for Butler to be able to announce that 'the Boxes will be the same price as when Mrs. Jordan and Miss Wallis performed here last season' that was 3/6d. Another notice requests Ladies and Gentlemen, in order to prevent confusion at the door, to send for tickets when they take places and to send servants in time to keep them. Another bill for 6th July advertises *The Beaux' Stratagem* and *Peeping Tom of Coventry* and a third for 8th July gives the *School for Scandal* with Butler as Sir Peter Teazle and Mrs. Tayleure as Lady Teazle followed by *Catherine and Petruchio*. Merchant, Cleland and Mrs. Hinde were newcomers.

The theatre reopened at Harrogate on 21st September when Miss Wallis on her way to Bath played Violante in *The Wonder* and the following day repeated *Amanthis*.[37] In the autumn this year Butler's company visited Thirsk and Lady Frankland wrote from Thirkleby Park to her sister Mrs. Courtney of Beverley on 14th October: 'I bespoke a Play, Mr. Butler's company being here. We had a very full house.'[38] Possibly Thirsk at that time was a regular circuit town because in an undated letter from Lady Frankland's daughter to her cousin Cornelius Courtney we read: 'I am sorry Butler don't come here this year as I like Plays very much'.

This winter Butler opened a new theatre in the Woolpack Yard in Kendal. J. F. Curwen[39] gives the date of this theatre as 1789, but Mr. Hogan has pointed out that according to the *Leeds Mercury* it was not yet functioning in July 1790.[40] Unlike the former one this playhouse had boxes which could be taken at the theatre each day from 10-1. The usual charges were made of boxes 3/-, pit 2/-, gallery 1/-. There was no admittance behind the scenes and no servants were admitted without payment. Mrs. Butler has a playbill for the New Theatre, Kendal, for 7th February 1791, on which date *The Maid of the Mill* and *Barnaby Brittle* were given for the benefit of Mrs. Martin.

We know nothing more of the players' fortunes and peregrinations until they returned to Beverley in 1791. An entry dated 30th May in John Courtney's diary reads:

> . . . at the Play for the Benefit of Mr. and Mrs. Tayleure, *The Battle of Hexham [,] Farm House*. Mr. Smith and I sat in the Stage Box (Prince Wales's).

On 10th June he went again:

> Benefit of Mr. and Mrs. Sandford. *Belle's Stratagem* and *Midnight Hour*. We sat in Front Seat of Front Box. Mr. Sandford acted very well.

Some playbills in the British Library give us some details of their season at Harrogate in 1791. On 16th July *She Stoops to Conquer* with Butler as Tony Lumpkin and Miss Hilliar as Miss Neville was followed by Jephson's new farce *Two Strings to Your Bow*, played here for the second time. On 20th July, *Inkle and Yarico* was played with Butler as Trudge followed by Macready's *Village Lawyer* for the first time.

On 23rd July, Mrs. Achmet was announced for two nights and played Clarinda in *The Suspicious Husband*. On this bill:

> Mr. Butler begs leave to inform the Ladies and Gentlemen at Harrogate, that Mr. Harley, of Covent Garden Theatre, (Successor to the late Mr. Henderson) has finished his Engagement at Richmond[41] where he has been performing a few Nights, with very great success, will make his first appearance here on Thursday next, in the Character of Shylock, in *The Merchant of Venice*.

For his second night on 30th July, he played Mortimer in *The Fashionable Lover* and was billed to play Macbeth later, and for his fifth night on 6th August he sustained Don Felix in *The Wonder*.[42]

For the benefit of Mr. and Mrs. Wright on 23rd August, O'Keeffe's *Wild Oats* was presented four months after it had appeared at Covent Garden, after which Wright played Harlequin to his wife's Columbine in a pantomime entitled *Mirth and Magic; or Harlequin's Revels* 'With new Scenery, Machinery, Dresses and Decorations. Harlequin's Metamorphoses, Escapes and Leaps with the Views of the Enchanted Grove, The Millers Shop. And Cupid's Garden'. A pantomime of this name was presented four years later at Astley's.

The following year Butler opened another new theatre at Ripon on 20th August 1792. On the opening night Miss Wallis played Calista; Amanthis and Portia on 21st and 22nd August, and Isabella in *Measure for Measure* on 24th August.[43] The theatre was built by George Hassell:

> . . . the scenery and decorations are excellent, and the manager endeavours to provide a respectable dramatic corps, with the novelties of the day, for the gratification of the public during the season.

The building was in Park Street on a site now occupied by the United Automobile Company's garage.[44]

The company's stay in Ripon must have been a short one because on Friday, 2nd September, they were performing for a week only at Richmond. In the Museum there is a petition from Samuel Butler from

Harrogate, 25th July, who proposed to open the Richmond Theatre on 23rd September and hoped their worships would grant him a licence. Our first Richmond playbill is for this date. On this occasion at least Miss Wallis played in her native town, and no less a character than Portia, though she was still only 18 years of age. W. Tayleure, though he played Old Gobbo, was probably the Tayleures' young son William. Wilkinson, Marriott and Todd are newcomers. A playbill for Harrogate for 23rd July 1793, gives Pilon's *He Would Be A Soldier* and O'Keeffe's *A Highland Reel*. New names are Tunstall, Bellair, Thorpe, Mrs. Wilkinson and Mr. and Mrs. Biggs whose benefit it was.

That Butler was flourishing is beyond doubt. In the winter of 1793 he took over Whitby and for many years made it his biennial winter headquarters. The theatre there in Scate Lane had been erected in 1784 as a successor to an older house in the Paddock on the west side of Cliff Lane. It held 500 people and was the property of the subscribers.[45] From 1784 until it was taken over by Butler in 1793, Whitby had been visited by Strickland's company. In its Museum is preserved an almost complete set of playbills for the years 1779 to 1818 when the Butler Company's tenure ended, and from these we are able to draw a great deal of information about the personnel of the company and the plays they performed.

The season was run as a subscription one for 21 nights, the box subscription being £2.2.0. and the pit £1.11.6. After that there was a series of benefits. The prices for individual performances were boxes 2/6d, pit 2/- and gallery 1/-. Tickets were to be had from Samuel Butler 'at Mr. Crofts, Painter, Baxtergate'. According to Butler's usual custom there was no admittance behind the scenes and no servants were admitted without payment. The playbill also announces that 'The Theatre is well aired, having had fires in it during the three weeks past.' Not only the cold but the press gang might act as a deterrent to theatre-going, so that a kind of truce was arranged and an announcement printed at the head of each playbill:

> Capt. Shortland pledges his word of honour that no seamen whatever shall be molested by his people on Playnights from the hour of four in the Afternoon to Twelve at night; after which time the indulgence ceases.

This enabled the sailors from the whaling fleet, who were good material for the press gang, to visit the theatre in safety.

The Whitby season opened on 2nd December 1793, and performances were given three nights a week. The last night, for Butler's benefit, was on 14th February 1794. The repertoire was a large one: 18 comedies, 8 comic operas, 7 musical or operatic farces, 7 pantomimes, 6 tragedies, 4 farces, 4 plays, 1 musical spectacle, and 1 burletta. The preponderance of comedy was a feature that persisted throughout the whole of Butler's regime in

Whitby and naturally reflects the situation in the London theatres. O'Keeffe was the most popular dramatist having 6 pieces performed, then came Shakespeare with 5 and Mrs. Inchbald and Colman the younger with 4 each. The Shakespeare plays were *Henry IV, Richard III, Merchant of Venice, Hamlet,* and *Romeo and Juliet.* An otherwise unknown entertainment *The Whitby Lasses* evidently had a local interest and appeal.

The company produced the following pieces that had first been presented in London in 1792; Mrs. Inchbald's *Everyone Has His Fault,* Reynolds's *How To Grow Rich,* Colman the Younger's *Mountaineers,* Hoare's *Prize,* as well as Preston's *Democratic Rage* which had been given only at the Crow Street Theatre, Dublin and *The Surrender at Valenciennes* which had appeared at Doncaster. The following pieces dated from 1792; Morton's *Columbus,* Holcroft's *Road to Ruin,* Pearce's *Hartford Bridge,* and Macready's *Irishman in London.* The company's resources then, enabled them to show Whitby many of the latest London successes.

Nor were effects lacking. Take for example the pantomime of *The Death of Captain Cook:*
> . . . with the Original Music, Scenery, Dresses and other Decorations. Part I. Consists of the Mode and Manners of the Islanders making Love. Omai's Choice; A View of the Altar; a Procession and Marriage. Dance of the Natives, and Single Combat. Part II. A View of the Sea, and Ship Resolution. Capt. Cook's Landing. The Reception given, and Presents offered to the Natives by Capt. Cook. A Savage Dance, and Battle of the Natives. Captain Cook's Death. Part III. Scene, a Morai, or Burying Place, the Funeral Procession of Captain Cook.

Members of the company were Butler, Tayleure and his son W. Tayleure, Wright, Baillie, Wilkinson, Martin, Sidney, Meadows, Macnally, Mackrall, Kewley, Francis, Mrs. Tayleure, Miss Tayleure, Mrs. Fildew, Mrs. Wright, Mrs. Hinde, Mrs. Martin, Mrs. Kay, Mrs. Wilkinson, Mrs. Mackrall. Of the newcomers the most noteworthy was Tom Meadows, who was to bring up his better known son Drinkwater Meadows (1799-1869) in the company. Walter Donaldson[46] tells us that:
> In this charming money getting circuit the Tayleurs and Meadowes were reared. The elder Meadows declared: 'After being attached to Theatres Royal in his time he never knew what real happiness was until he came to this circuit.'

Two more Tayleure children Master John and Miss Tayleure played Ben and Miss Prue in a scene from *Love for Love.*

From Whitby the company proceeded to Ripon where they opened on 19th February with the *Road to Ruin* and *Babes In The Wood.* The playbill for this occasion is at Whitby and was evidently printed there in order to be ready to distribute on arrival after the long journey. From Ripon the company went on to Beverley. John Courtney records three visits this year after an absence from the theatre of two years. The first was on 26th May 1794:

> Benefit of Mr. and Mrs. Wilkinson. *The West Indian* and *The Beverley Lasses.* New and most absurd. A tollerable house.

The Beverley Lasses was presumably an adaptation to Beverley of *The Whitby Lasses.* The second visit is recorded on 2nd June:

> Benefit of Mr. Francis and Mr. – *Beaux Stratagem* and *Castle Of Andalusia*, new and pretty. There was a party from the Hall there and several Officers of the Northumberland Militia – Mr. Francis having been a Lt.Col. 'tis said.'

For his third visit on 11th June, it was the:

> Benefit of Mr. and Mrs. Wright. *Widow of Malabar*, and *The Ghost* and *Harlequin's Invasion.*

From Beverley the company doubtless progressed to Harrogate and Richmond. By 1st December they were acting in Kendal. Mrs. Butler has a playbill for this date on which Morton's *Columbus* was given there for the first time. The scenic effects included an Indian procession, a new scene of the Temple of the Sun which is destroyed by a hurricane and discovers the eruption of a volcano and Columbus's triumphal entry attended by Spaniards, Monks, Prisoners, Banners, and Trophies. The afterpiece was O'Keeffe's comic opera *Fontainbleau.* William Tayleure's wife was now acting and other new names are Townsend, Montagu and Mrs. Macnally.

The company returned to Beverley in May 1795. On 29th May, Courtney was again 'at the Play – *By Desire* of Lt. Gen. Scott, The Dramatist and Mock Doctor.' On 13th June, he records: 'I and my Son were at a Concert Benefit of Mr. Tayleure. My Son danced.'

Our next information is from the second Whitby season of 1795-6. The subscription for 21 nights had been reduced in price, the boxes falling from 2 guineas to £1.10.0. and the pit from £1.11.6. to £1.2.6. The season opened on 18th November,the benefits began on 1st January, and the last night of playing was on 9th February. During this time the company performed 19 comedies, 10 farces, 7 musical or operatic farces, 7 tragedies, 6 melodramas, 3 plays, 3 comic operas, 2 pantomimes, 2 interludes and a musical entertainment.

Melodrama was beginning its long and popular career and Butler was not behind the times in providing for the popular taste. There were also more farces and less comic operas than during the previous season. O'Keeffe retained his place as the most popular dramatist, having ten pieces performed; Shakespeare was second with five, and Cumberland third with four. The Shakespeare plays were *Othello* and *Macbeth* in which Butler played the title roles, *As You Like It, Henry IV* and *The Merchant of Venice.*

22

On 13th January, a strange concoction of wonders was produced which is otherwise unknown. It was called *Les Ombres Impalpables or The Whimsical School of Proteus, a Harlequinade*. The synopsis is worth quoting in full:

Columbine's flight to the skies pursued by Harlequin, Clown, Pantaloon, Scaramouche and Frenchman. He mounts his magic sword and ascends in search of her. A parcel of grotesque figures. The surprising jumpers. The miraculous climbers. Several Hogarthian caricatures of several forms, shapes, sizes. Two determined card players descending from a cloud; play at All Fours; dispute the game; quarrel ensues; They strip and box it out; During the battle the modern science of various pugilisms will be displayed as practised by Mendoza, Big Ben and other amateurs of the profession. The Witch of Endor comes wheeling round in a whirlwind accompanied by thunder, lightening and rain; she touches the whimsical little man with her rod who from a dwarf of 18 inches suddenly rises to the astonishing height of 12 feet and by one stride seems to step the distance of gallery from stage. The extraordinary tooth drawer performs the operation with calipers and extracts from mouth of patient a tooth of most enormous size. To conclude with an aerial dance of the characters.

The exhibitions and feats of the fair were thus brought into the theatre. No less than 16 other new plays were performed; new to London in 1795 were Andrews's *Mysteries of the Castle*, Cumberland's *Wheel of Fortune*, O'Keeffe's *Irish Mimic* and *Life's Vagaries*, Holcroft's *Deserted Daughter*, Harlstone's *Crotchet Lodge*, Morton's *Zorinski*; new to London in 1794 were Arnold's *Auld Robin Gray*, Reynolds's *Rage*, Waldron's *Heigho for a Husband*, Cross's *Purse* and *Apparition*, Boaden's *Fontainville Forest*, Pearce's *Netley Abbey*, Mrs. Cowley's *Town Before You* and Mrs. Inchbald's *Wedding Day*.

A Mrs. Inchbald, probably the wife of George Inchbald stepson of the authoress, had joined the company as an actress and was advertised as from the Theatre Royal, Haymarket. She evidently did not stay with them long, as there is no mention of her name the following year. Other newcomers were Mr. and Mrs. Clarke from Edinburgh, Mr. and Mrs. Maxwell, Davis, Cottrell from Dublin and Mrs. Meadows.

The company opened at Ripon on 13th February, four days after they left Whitby, with *The Jew* and *Sprigs of Laurel*. Whilst at Ripon Butler quarrelled with the Tayleures as Cuitt relates in a letter to Canon Tate dated 9th May 1796 (in Mr. Wenham's possession):

I must now tell you something of a terrible kick up that has happen'd amongst the Players at Ripon the fact is as far as I could learn that the Tayleures had fail'd in their benefits in consequence of which they wanted to have fresh ones to which it seems Butler was not agreeable therefore the Tayleures were determined to quit the Company and set up for themselves that there has been a quarrel I suppose is beyond a doubt but I think in the end matters will be made up as it is not the Interest of either party to quarrel. Tayleure it seems had a Concert but how it succeeded with regard to profit I have not yet learned.

[He had had a concert benefit at Beverley in 1795.] Whether the Tayleures did leave for a while I do not know; but their names do not appear in a Beverley playbill for 6th May 1796.[47] However they were with the company again in 1797 and stayed on until 1801. The Beverley bill announces the first performance there of Cumberland's comedy *First Love* which had been presented in London in 1795. Mrs. Inchbald played Lady Ruby and Butler David Mowbray. The afterpiece was *The Apprentice*.

Elections took place at Beverley towards the end of the month and the two candidates regaled their supporters with free performances. On Friday, 28th May, John Courtney enters in his diary; 'I went with Col. Burton to the Play and we went on the Stage. He gave a Play (gratis) tonight' and on 28th May he adds 'Mr. Tatton gave a Free Play on Thursday and Mr. Burton on Friday night.'

Jane Wallis returned to play for one night and Courtney patronised the performance which was on 9th June:

Miss Wallis performed for one Night – *Every One Has His Fault* – Lady Eleanor Irwin by Miss Wallis; who performed it charmingly and made many People cry. The Farce was *My Grandmother*. The Boxes were 3 shills. The House was quite full – I got a back seat in the Pr. Wales's Stage Box – it was the same Place I sat in when I last saw Miss Wallis near six years ago, [To the very day, 9th June 1790. Cornelius died soon afterwards] when my poor Son Cornelius was at the Play at the far end of the same Side Box when it was most excessively Hot.

We have a glimpse of the company at Kendal in the spring of 1797 from a paragraph in the *Monthly Mirror*[48]: They opened there with *The Wheel of Fortune*, and *The Way to Get Married* and *Fortune's Fool* were repeated with great applause. Butler as Dashall and Tom Seymour, Wright as Tangent and Aphazard, Meadows as Toby Allspice and Sir Bramber Blackletter, Clark as Capt. Faulkner, Davis as Caustic, Mrs. W. Tayleure as Clementina; Mrs. Fildew as Lady Sorrel and Miss Union are picked out for commendation. Mrs. Inchbald played Lady Danvers and Julia Faulkner, but the critic advises her, since she was no longer in the bloom of youth, to think less of herself. Of Townsend the less said the better. The band was under the direction of the Messrs. Tayleures and was well conducted. To sum up 'the whole company, with a few exceptions, is equal, if not superior, to most in the country, and reflects credit on the liberality of the manager'.

24

In Beverley in 1797 Courtney visited the theatre twice: 5th May '*A Cure For The Heartache* and *First Floor*. The Play was a new and very good one and a merry one from beginning to end, and in general well acted.' (Morton's comedy had been first given at Covent Garden on 10th January that year). 31st May, 'Benefit of Mr. and Mrs. Wright. *He Wd Be A Soldier* and *Harlequin Fortunatus*.'

In September 1797 Butler suffered a personal loss in the death of his wife, Tryphosa, at the age of 70. After her third marriage to Butler she does not seem to have taken an active part, and her name does not occur in any playbill, but to her the company owed its continued existence for many years, and her death must have meant to them the passing of an era in their history.

In this same year Frances Maria Jefferson, who was to become Butler's second wife, joined the company from Exeter. She was the daughter of Thomas Jefferson, a native of Ripon and a well known actor and theatrical manager.[49] For many years he had been sole, and then part, proprietor of the Plymouth Theatre which he had, however, quitted in 1795/6. In 1767 he married as his second wife the daughter of Mrs. Bainbridge, an actress at Covent Garden, and by her he had six children. His son Joseph emigrated to America and was the first of the series of famous American actors of that name. Three of his other children, George, Frances Maria and Elizabeth, were to be connected with the Richmond Company.

We first hear of Miss Jefferson when the company was in Harrogate in July and there she played Mrs. Oakley in *The Jealous Wife*, Lady Danvers in Reynolds's *Fortune's Fool*, Lady Bab Lardoon in *The Maid of the Oaks*, Emily Tempest in *The Wheel of Fortune*, Roxalana in *The Sultan*, these two last for her benefit, Juliana Faulkner in *The Way to Get Married* and Augusta Aubrey in *The Fashionable Lover*. She was therefore playing leading parts as soon as she joined the company. Other newcomers were Miss Miles, Thompson from Edinburgh and Fawcett. Butler himself played Major Oakley in *The Jealous Wife*, Tom Seymour in *Fortune's Fool* for his benefit, Tempest in *The Wheel of Fortune*, Dickey Dashall in *The Way to get Married* and Colin Macleod in *The Fashionable Lover*. As was very usual a local flavour was given to one of the interludes, *Tony Lumpkin's Ramble* (O'Keeffe's piece was also altered to suit Whitby and this version is printed in Meadows's *Thespian Gleanings*) recited by Meadows including 'his Journey to Harrogate – Description of Knaresborough – the Dropping Well – St. Robert's Chapel etc.' The company were in Harrogate during July and August then, doubtless, proceeded for their autumn season, to Richmond. In October they suffered another loss in the death of Juliana Wright, wife of James Brockell Wright, who had played with the company for at least eight years. She is buried in Richmond Churchyard and her tombstone states that she 'departed this life, Oct. 9th, 1797. Aged 31.'

The Whitby season for winter 1797-8 opened on 15th November, the benefits started on 1st January, and the last performance took place on 16th February. The subscription was boxes £1.16.0. pit £1.7.0. for 15 nights, a considerable increase in price on the previous season. The boxes, we learn, had been newly papered and lined and the whole painted in elegant style.

A feature of the repertoire was the increased proportion of tragedies performed, though comedy still held a vast preponderance; there were fewer melodramas and more comic operas given than in the previous season. The figures are – comedies 25, tragedies 12, farces 11, musical or operatic farces 7, comic operas 6, melodramas 3, pantomimes 2, musical entertainment, play and interlude 1. For the first time O'Keeffe is not among the most popular playwrights, but the list is headed by Morton with 6 pieces. Shakespeare retains second place with 5, and Cumberland, Hoare and Bickerstaffe each have 4. W. Butler played principal roles in the Shakespeare plays appearing as Hamlet, with Samuel as the first gravedigger, as Romeo, Richard III and Lear. *The Merchant of Venice* was also played. Other pre-18th century revivals were *A New Way to Pay Old Debts, Oroonoko, Mourning Bride, Venice Preserv'd, Every man His Humour, Rival Queens;* Morton's *Secrets Worth Knowing* was presented on the last night (16th February) less than five weeks after its presentation at Covent Garden.

Other new plays were Colman the Younger's *Heir At Law*, Morton's *Cure For The Heart Ache*, Mrs. Inchbald's *Wives As they Were*, T. Knight's *Honest Thieves*, Cumberland's *False Impressions* which had all been brought out in London 1797, and Reynolds's *Fortune's Fool*, Morton's *Way To Get Married*, Holman's *Abroad and At Home*, Holcroft's *Man of Ten Thousand*, Brewer's *Bannion Day*, and Birch's *Smugglers* first seen in London in 1796.

What relation, if any, W. Butler was to Samuel I do not know. He played leading parts but did not stay with the company long as his name does not appear in cast lists after 1800. Other new names are Stackwood from Worcester, Mrs. Hargrave from Plymouth and Mrs. Baillie. On 7th February it was announced that 'Tickets delivered by Mr. Henry Tayleure, Mast. J. Tayleure, The Hair Dresser, the Stage Keeper will be admitted.' Henry Tayleure was probably another son of the elder Tayleure's. It is interesting to note that among the lesser lights the hairdresser was not forgotten.

John Courtney saw the company perform in Beverley on 30th May 1798. 'By desire *Grammar School, Castle Spectre* new, and *The Invasion*. I sat in the Pit and was entertained.' On 14th June some of his party were:
> . . . at the Play in a Seat taken off from the Pit. Mr. Gilbey and I went just behind them and sat in the Front Box. They did not stay the Entertainment.

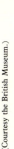

MAHOMET.

Act III.   *Scene I.*

De Wilde pinxt   *Long Sculpt*

MISS WALLIS as PALMIRA.

Plate IV. *Jane Wallis as Palmira
in Miller's Mahomet the Imposter.*

MISS WALLIS as ASPASIA.

Plate V. *Jane Wallis as Aspasia
in Samuel Johnson's Irene.*

(Courtesy the British Museum.)

LAST NIGHT

OF PERFORMANCE

NEW THEATRE, THIRSK.

On Saturday Evening, October 2nd, 1819,

Will be presented the Celebrated Comedy of

A Cure for the

HeartAche.

Written by T. MORTON, Esq. Author of Speed the Plough, the School of Reform, &c

Sir Hubert Stanley,..........................Mr GEORGE
Charles Stanley,...............................Mr. ALEXANDER
Old Rapid,....................Mr. SAUNDERS....................Young Rapid, Mr BUTLER
Bronze,.,..........Mr. BROWN...........Waiter Mr STOKER
Farmer Oatland,.......Mr. WOOD.........Frank Oatland Mr. HODGSON
Jes-y Oatland,.........Miss BUTLER
Miss. Vortex,......Mrs. HODGSON.......Elen Vortex,......Mrs SAUNDERS

End of the Play,

The Nightingale Club

By Mr. JEFFERSON.

A COMIC SONG

By Mr. WOOD.

The whole to conclude with a new Farce, called

High Notions.

Sir Frederick Augustus Pageant Bart {just come to the title by the } Mr. SANDERS
{ eath of his brother. }
Mr Franklin, (a gentleman in love with Miss Pageant) Mr ALEXANDER
Brisk, (Franklin's servant a sharp, clever fellow) Mr BUTLER
Timothy, (Sir Frederick's Factotum, Valet, Cook. Butler, &c.) ....Mr JEFFERSON.
Head Waiters, Waiters, Servants, &c.

Charlotte (Sir Frederick's Niece, an accomplished Young Lady) Miss BUTLER
Martha, (her waiting woman, a fantastical girl fond of dress, &c) ....Mrs HODGSON
Mrs O'Conner (Landlady of the Inn)......Mrs WOOD

Doors to be opened at 6 and performance to commence at 7 o'clock.

Boxes 3s. Pit 2s. Gal. 1s.

Tickets to be had at the Printing Office.

Masterman, Printer, Thirsk,

Plate VI.   New Theatre, Thirsk: 2nd October, 1819.

Two Harrogate bills for this summer are in the British Library. They record the production for the first time there of Reynolds's *Laugh When You Can* and Colman the Younger's *Blue Beard* 'with new Scenery and Machinery, New Dresses and appropriate Decorations. The Original Chorusses and Marches' on 27th July; and the second performance of Sheridan's *Pizarro* on 29th August. From them we learn of the following additions to the company: Roberts, Bennett, Lewis, Mason, Mr. and Mrs. Darley and Mr. and Mrs. Francis.

Courtney's entry for the 1799 season at Beverley is brief: 15th May 'Went to the Play *Lovers' Vows.*' In Harrogate the rope dancer Saxoni appeared for two nights.[50] I have been unable to discover any Richmond playbills for these years but among Canon Tate's papers there is one dated 21st November 1797, for a performance, not at the theatre but at the Low School, for the benefit of Mrs. Darley who was a member of the company.

The pieces performed were George Colman the younger's *New Hay At The Old Market* and an otherwise unknown farce entitled *The Good Son*. The women's parts were played by the boys, and charges were boxes 2/-, pit 1/-. The occasion and result of the benefit are described in a letter from the Rev. James Tate, then headmaster of Richmond School, to Mrs. Ottley, dated 23rd November 1799:

> And now I come to tell you of a very good thing done by our boys this week. Mrs. Darley the wife of Mr. Darley, one of Mr. Butler's company, was confined the very morning on which the company left for Whitby. Here she was left with two children besides, & indeed to do justice to the good people of the town & neighbourhood they were not wanting in their attentions to her –. Well amongst our boys my own scholars that board in the house particularly, Mrs. Darley's distress was mentioned when a thought struck one of them, which was heartily embraced by the rest, that they would act a play in the school for her benefit, of course my consent was soon obtained & my hearty concurrence too. On Wednesday night the curtain drew up, I should have said arose, to a very fashionable crowded audience Lady Audley, Miss Touchet, Mr. & Mrs. Bell of Easby, Mrs. Mair of the Hill House, Mrs. Duff, Mrs. Dunbar, Miss Weir, the Claghills & as many more, and yesterday morning Margaret carried a note from the scholars to Mrs. Darley enclosing a five guinea bill, which was most gratefully received & must be truly acceptable, as she has to travel near sixty miles at this hard season betwixt this & Whitby. Besides this the expenses of the house were defrayed & twelve shillings given amongst some distressed persons in the town. I must not forget to say that I drew up a prologue at a very hasty notice.

This incident is further evidence of the personal interest the townspeople took in the players, and of the practical sympathy that any distress among them evoked. The link between the school and the comedians must have been strengthened by the fact that the headmaster had married into the Wallis family.

So we return to Whitby in 1799-1800. The season opened in mid November and concluded on 21st February. On one occasion the Whitby new band performed in the orchestra; but of even greater local interest was the production of a play by a Whitby dramatist. Francis Gibson's *Streanstall Abbey* was first presented on 2nd December 1799, and was given the honour of a second performance on 13th December, and a third on 12th February 1800. Gibson was Collector of Customs and his five-act, blank-verse, historical play has, according to the *Biographia Dramatica* 'considerable merit, and is well calculated to promote sentiments of virtue and patriotism.' It was printed in 1800. Gibson's *Poetical Remains*, 1807 contain three addresses and one song delivered at the theatre, but probably before the Butler regime since one address is dated 1787.

This season the company gave 26 comedies, 13 farces, 8 comic operas, 7 tragedies, 6 melodramas, 6 musical or operatic farces, 5 plays, 2 interludes, 2 ballad operas and 1 musical entertainment. Six pieces by Colman the younger, 5 by Shakespeare and O'Keeffe and 4 by Thomas Dibdin, Sheridan, Bickerstaffe and Mrs. Inchbald were acted. The Shakespeare plays were the same as the previous year. Plays that had been first seen in London in 1799 were Morris's *Secret*, Charlotte Smith's *What Is She?* Thomas Dibdin's *Five Thousand a Year* and *Birthday*, T. Knight's *Turnpike Gate*, Reynolds's *Management*; those first seen in London in 1798 were Mrs. Inchbald's *Lovers' Vows*, Colman the younger's *Blue Beard*, Thomas Dibdin's *Jew and the Doctor*, Thompson's *Stranger*, Oulton's *Botheration*, Reynold's *Laugh When You Can*. A Master Meadows makes his appearance during this season.

In a note in the last playbill of the season Butler returned thanks for all favours 'and in particular the attention paid him in his Benefit'; he also begged leave to inform the public that:

> . . . it has been a universal complaint, there not being a proper distinction between the Price of Boxes and Pit as 3s is common in almost every Theatre in the kingdom, Mr. Butler hopes that the ladies and gentlemen of Whitby will not think it improper if in future Boxes here be the same. No alteration will be made in regard to subscription tickets.

That is the theatre was sufficiently prosperous for Butler to raise the box seats from 2/6d to 3/-.

After leaving Whitby the company proceeded as usual to Ripon. There is a playbill of this season in Ripon[51] dated Saturday, 22nd March 1800 'By desire of the Ladies and Gentlemen of the Assembly', advertising Monk

Lewis's famous melodrama *The Castle Spectre* for the second time:

with a variety of scenery and machinery, particularly Portraits, Armoury, Sliding Panels, Grand Oratory, Subterranean dungeon, Transparencies etc. etc.

all the paraphernalia in fact of the pseudo-Gothic romance. The puff continues:

It is almost needless to inform the public of the uncommon number of nights *The Castle Spectre* has been acted to crowded houses in London[52] and still commands the same attraction whenever it is repeated. Mr. Butler assures his friends that he has not spared any expense to render the said piece worthy of the approbation and support.

The cast was Osmond – Stackwood, Reginald – W. Butler, Percy – Darley, Father Philip – Meadows, Motley – Bennett, Kenrick – George, Saib – Roberts, Hassan – Francis, Muley – Lewis, Alaric – Fawcett, Allan – Martin, Eric – Townsend, Angela – Miss Jefferson, Alice – Mrs. Fildew, Castle Spectre – Miss Miles. The farce was *High Life Below Stairs* in which Butler played Lovel, George – Freeman, and Roberts Lord Duke. When the company was in Beverley Courtney paid them several visits which are thus recorded in his diary:

19th May.

Management a Comedy – Bad one – *St. Patrick's Day or the Scheming Lieutenant* – pretty good entertainment.

21st May.

I and my Wife and our two daughters were at the Play. *Heir At Law* and *Blue Beard* new. I was very well entertained. The Scenery and Machinery in *Blue Beard* were very pretty but these wanted music.

6th June.

I and my Wife and Daughters were at the Play and my sons John and Thos. came in at the Half Price – *Way To Get Married* and *All The World's a Stage*. Good Play and well acted. By desire of the Grammar School.

9th June.

I was at the Play by desire of Free Masons. *The Stranger* and *Deserter*. I did not like the Play neither in seeing it acted or in reading. It was well got up.

13th June.

. . . at the Play for Benefit of Mr. Bennett. We sat in Front Box.

16th June. The play of *The Mountaineers* was over by the time Courtney reached the theatre:

The farces were a *Trip to Scotland* and the *Jew and the Doctor* for the Benefit of Mr. and Mrs. Meadows – there was a pretty good House.

18th June.
    Benefit of Mr. Martin and Mrs. Fildew. *Battle of Hexham* and *The Purse*.

By the time the company had reached Harrogate in July Butler had married Frances Maria Jefferson. She appears as Mrs. Butler on 8th July in the role of Juliana in Reynolds's *Management* and on 17th July she played Caroline Dormer in *The Heir at Law*.[53] *Management, Speed the Plough,* Dibdin's *St. David's Day* and Thompson's adaptation from Kotzebue, *The Stranger*, were among the new pieces presented at this Harrogate season. According to a report in *The Monthly Mirror*[54]:

> In point of regularity and respectability the performance was equal to those of most provincial companies, and the scenery, dresses and decorations reflect great credit on the care, taste and liberality of the manager.

On 6th October 1800, Butler opened another new theatre, this time at Northallerton, with a performance of *Pizarro*,[55] the Sheridan adaptation of Kotzebue's tragedy. Northallerton had been mentioned as a circuit town by Fielding Wallis as far back as 1787, though where the company then played we do not know. The theatre that Butler built in 1800 still exists though it has been quite dismantled and now serves as a slaughterhouse.

The occasional prologue spoken at the opening of the new theatre by Tom Meadows and written by Cross and Dibdin junior is printed in Tom Meadows's *Thespian Gleanings*[56] Part of it, jumbled with another piece printed from the same source, is reprinted in J. L. Saywell, *History and Annals of Northallerton*.[57] After declaring that it is . . .

    'our constant aim
    By assiduity to gain a name
    Your approbation points the road to Fame –

And that –

    'Your fiat must our future fates control,
    For here our chief has "garner'd up his soul"
    Eager to please, his throbbing heart beats high,
    By you depress'd or swell'd to extacy.'

he appeals, as was customary, to –

    'Ye fair who gaily circling sit,
    The galaxy of beauty, and of wit,
    Or you gay goddesses, who lofty tow'r,
    And urge the laughing gods to cry encore'

for –

    'Critic man will applaud, if beauty takes the lead.'

So Butler started the new century with a new wife and a new theatre.

CHAPTER III

The Last Years of Samuel Butler, the Elder, 1800 – 1812

ON 14TH DECEMBER 1800, James Brockhill Wright, an infant son of 'Mr. Wright, Comedian' was buried at Ulverston.[58] This is the first indication we have that Ulverston was now in Butler's circuit. Exactly when he took it over we do not know. Harriot Mellon had made her first appearance on the stage there in Bibby's company in 1787, and in 1792 and 1794 Ross was the manager of the company.[59] In 1796 a new theatre[60] was erected by subscription on the tontine system, and it is tempting to conjecture that it was built for Butler's first season there, but of this we have no positive evidence. Henceforward together with Kendal it was visited by Butler in alternate years.

Mrs. Butler possesses several Kendal playbills for the 1800-1801 season. The first is for 26th December 1800 on which is recorded the first performance of *Laugh when you Can* followed by Saxoni's feats on the tight rope. He had been engaged by Butler for three nights and his last performance and benefit was on 31st December after the first performance of Mrs. Inchbald's *Wise Man of the East* and *The Maid of the Oaks*. Other plays new to Kendal given during the season were *Blue Beard*, *The Castle Spectre*, *Saint David's Day*, *Obi*, *Sighs*, *Fortune's Frolic* and *Life*. A ballet called *The Frenchman's Mistake* was put on with elaborate scenery including:

> . . . a grand emblematic transparent Painting of Sedition and Rebellion Chained by Britannia supporting the Crown of England – Lord Nelson after the glorious Battle of the Nile, receiving the Sword of the French Admiral on Board the Vanguard – Peace seated on a Globe supported by Neptune and Mars, with a Medallion of Lord Duncan.

Keys, a newcomer who was only to remain with the company a year, played

Macbeth to the Lady Macbeth of Mrs. Butler and Richard III to Mrs. Butler's Queen. Other newcomers were Wright's second wife, formerly Mrs. Dunn, and Mrs. Butler's brother George Jefferson who was to be one of the company's most staunch supporters. The season closed at Kendal on 13th March and by May Butler was back in Beverley.

John Courtney gives the following reports in his diary:

4th May.
> *Deaf and Dumb* and *Fortune's Frolick*.[61] Both new – entertained with both pretty well. We were at the Play very often.

11th May.
> By desire of Grammar School. *Life*, new, and *Obi* a Pantomime, new[62] and the most tiresome thing I ever saw. Above half past 11 when we came away.

18th May.
> *Pizarro* and *High Life Below Stairs*. I went merely because Mrs. Beverley bespoke it, for I dislike the Play, and was sadly tired indeed, it was miserably acted, especially Butler's Rolla. I was entertained with the old Farce I had so often seen.

His disgruntlement did not prevent his paying further visits to the theatre:

10th June.
> *Wild Oats* and *Paul and Virginia* both new.

19th June.
> At the Play at Half Price. *Cure for the Heart Ache* and *Wags of Windsor*.

23rd June.
> The Play was *Hamlet* (by Butler) and *Spoil'd Child*. The Play terribly acted.

26th June.
> *The Lie of a Day* and *Prisoner at Large*.

The diarist had never before been so severe on the company's abilities, but whether it was because he was a tired and troubled man or whether the standard of acting had indeed deteriorated we cannot now tell.

Some Harrogate playbills of 1801 range from 2nd July to 5th August but do not, of course, cover the extent of the season. Among those who bespoke evenings were the Countesses of Home, Ormond and Shaftesbury, Lady Castlereagh and Mrs. Goldie. Performances began at 7 p.m. and box places were to be had of Butler at the theatre: 'Tickets Deliver'd when places taken.' Some bills request those who have taken places to send servants in time to keep them. Among the pieces new to Harrogate were Fawcett's pantomime *Obi*, Colman the Younger's musical farce *The Wags of Windsor* (usually known as *The Review*), Prince Hoare's comedy *Indiscretion*, Thomas Dibdin's musical farce *Of Age To-morrow* and his farce *The Jew and The Doctor*, Reynolds's comedy *Folly As It Flies* and Cross's pantomime *Black Beard*.

The scenery for *Obi* was painted by Tayleure. A synopsis of the scenery for *Pizarro* is given on the bill: 'With scenery, Dresses, &c – The Scenery, – Pizarro's Tent – Temple of the Sun – Falling Bridge – Mountainous Country, – Dungeon, – Cascade &c'; in Act II there was a procession of Peruvians, vocal parts by Darley, Wright, Mrs. Tayleure, Miss Jefferson, Mrs. Murray, &c. and in Act V. 'A Solemn Dirge at the Death and Funeral of Rolla, by Priests and Priestesses of the Sun.'

But perhaps the highlight of the season was John Bannister's starring visit for two nights. On 30th July he played Marplot in *The Busy Body* and Frederick in *Of Age To-morrow*, stated on the bill to be his own translation from Kotzebue, but usually attributed to Thomas Dibdin. On 1st August he acted Acres in *The Rivals* with the following cast: Sir Anthony Absolute – Meadows, Capt. Absolute – Wright, Faulkland – Darley, Sir Lucius O'Trigger – Murray, Fag – Webber, David – Jefferson, Mrs. Malaprop – Mrs. Fildew, Lydia Languish – Mrs. Tayleure, Julia – Mrs. Darley, Lucy – Mrs. Murray; he afterwards took the part of Will Steady in Cross's farce *The Purse*.

Let us consider for a moment the changes which had taken place in the company. Mrs. Butler made her first appearance this season rather late as Lady Townley in *The Provok'd Husband* on 4th August. It is possible that before she was engaged in giving birth to her daughter[63] though this is mere conjecture. In the meantime as well as her brother George Jefferson, her sister Elizabeth Jefferson had joined the company and henceforward the Jefferson family was to play a major part in its affairs. Of Butler's first wife's family, the Tayleures remained but left after this year; their son and his wife, the W. Tayleures, had already departed. Butler himself played frequently, taking such parts as Dr. Pangloss in *The Heir at Law*, O'Whack (with an Irish French Song) in *Notoriety*, Caleb Quotem in *The Wags of Windsor*, Sir Francis Gripe in *The Busy Body*, Lord Townley in *The Provok'd Husband*, Abednego in *The Jew and the Doctor* and Rolla in *Pizarro*. He took his benefit on 6th August and secured a well attended house.[64] W. Butler's name does not appear henceforth. Of the old stagers, George, the Martins and Mrs. Fildew were still going strong, as also were the Darleys and the Meadowses. Newcomers were the Murrays, Mrs. Murray remaining as one of the company's leading ladies until 1819. Among the children a Master Meadows, Master D. (Drinkwater) Meadows and a Master Hinde are mentioned. In *Obi* Master Hinde played Quashee's Child and Master D. Meadows Sam's Child, whilst to Master Meadows was assigned the role of the Page in *The Purse*.

And now for the first time for many years we have a glimpse of the company in Richmond in October. The Lennox Lodge of Freemasons visited the Theatre during that month to see Morton's *Secrets Worth Knowing*.[65] On 30th October a benefit was given in the following sad circumstances related in a letter from the Rev. James Tate to his mother dated 29th October:

> You may have heard that poor Willy Wright the carpenter, in a fit of melancholy put an end to himself a few months ago – Not long after, his second son was working inside the Playhouse, fell from a great height, and bruised his side, poor fellow, and broke his arm. He is now recovering and Mr. Butler gives him a benefit tomorrow night – which may serve, as his poor mother says, to pay a long Doctor's bill, and help him a little for the time he has been out of work, and the expense he has been at, in his illness.

We may hope that the benefit was a success and that Wright's troubles were eased by Butler's generous action.

The Whitby season opened on 18th November 1801 for an 18 nights' subscription, boxes £1.16.0., pit £1.7.0. As proposed the previous season the individual box tickets were now 3/-, the pit remained at 2/- and the gallery 1/-, the prices being thus aligned with those charged at Harrogate. The season closed on 19th February 1802. West, the dancer, was engaged for four nights only from 14th December to appear between the play and the farce during which time nothing under full price was taken. For his benefit a special *ballet d'action* entitled *The Muse's Chaplet*, in which he danced with the company, was given. On 12th February the Masons bespoke an evening and the company honoured the occasion by a special piece of scenery, a transparency, emblematical of masonry, painted by Thwaites 'Seen through Arches, and supported by Companions Butler, Wright, Martin and Brother Murray.' It was not at all unusual for actors to be masons and masonic lodges were generally loyal and generous supporters of the players. Local talent was encouraged not only by the revival of Gibson's *Streanstall Abbey* but by the production of a new tragedy by another native of Whitby. On 15th February, William Watkins's *The Fall of Carthage* first saw the light of the stage, though part of it had been written in 1778-9, when the author was 24, and the remainder about 1794.[66] The cast was as follows: Asdrubal – Keys, Harro – Murray, Adherbal – Davis, Bostar – George, Mago – Fawcett, Hiempsal – Fenton, Massilius – Jefferson, Annibal and Amilcar (children) – Master Meadows and D. Meadows, Bomilcar – Megget, Phoenissa – Mrs. Butler, Barce – Mrs. Wright, Scipio – Wright, Metellus – Darley, Mancinus – Webber, Marius – Meadows, Micipsa – Martin; the prologue was spoken by Darley and the epilogue by Mrs. Wright. Watkins dedicated the published play to Mrs. Butler:

. . . whose excellent performance of the principal personage in this drama, impresses the writer with admiration of her talents, and gratitude for her exertion of them.

He speaks too in his Proem of 'the general approbation bestowed upon the first theatrical performance of the following Tragedy' and expresses his obligation to Gibson 'whose friendship accelerated its actual production.' The company comes in for its share of praise:

The liberal conduct of the Manager of the Theatre, in accepting and preparing this Tragedy for representation, and the general attention of the Performers in the Parts allotted them at the time of acting it, merit the thanks of its Author.

Among the subscribers to the publication are named S. Butler 6 copies, Mrs. Butler 2, Thomas Meadows and Francis Murray. Twenty-four comedies, 11 farces, 8 musical farces, 6 comic operas, 5 plays and tragedies, 4 pantomimes, 3 melodramas and 2 musical entertainments were presented. Shakespeare figured but poorly, only *Macbeth, The Merchant of Venice* and *Richard III* being played. This was the high time of the craze for translations and adaptations from Kotzebue's plays and the company responded by presenting *Pizarro, The Stranger, Lovers' Vows, Of Age To-morrow, Sighs* and *The Wise Man of the East.* Seven pieces by O'Keeffe, six by Thomas Dibdin and Colman the Younger and five by Reynolds were performed. Plays new to London in 1801 were Colman the Younger's *Poor Gentleman,* Thomas Dibdin's *School for Prejudice,* Holcroft's *Deaf and Dumb,* Reynolds's *Folly As It Flies;* new to London in 1800 were Allingham's *'Tis All A Farce,* Kemble's *Point of Honour,* Hoare's *Indiscretion,* Reynolds's *Life,* Thomas Dibdin's *St. David's Day,* Cobb's *Paul and Virginia,* Fawcett's *Obi* and Colman the Younger's *Wags of Windsor.* Fenton and Meggett were new actors. Miss Wright and Miss Darley who took part in the pantomime *Black Beard* were evidently children.

The following entries in John Courtney's diary relate to the company's season at Beverley in 1802:

17th May.

At the Play (by Desire of Mayor and Corporation). *Cure for the Heartache* and *Turnpike Gate.*

28th May.

By Desire of Grammar School. *The Poor Gentleman* (new and pretty good) and *Who's the Dupe?* Good House.

10th June.

At the Play (By Desire of the Stewards).[67] We went into the Play House in the 2nd Act. I never saw the Boxes and Pit fuller. We were obliged to sit at the end of the Far Side Box, next Door; it was very hot, noisy and desperately crowded – we came away before the Farce.

It does not sound very comfortable but was evidently very alive and successful.

From Beverley the company moved to their summer season at Harrogate. They were playing there on 17th July when Colman the Younger's *Poor Gentleman* was given for the second time. Reynolds's *Folly As It Flies* was also given here this season for the first time. Miss de Camp acted with the company for three nights; on 10th August she played Hypolita in *She Wou'd and She Wou'd Not*, and Maria in *Of Age To-morrow*; on 12th August she was Lady Teazle to Butler's Sir Peter, and Little Pickle (with songs) in *The Spoil'd Child*.

There are five more entries in Courtney's diary for the Beverley season in 1803 which reveal it as a most successful one:

9th May.

I and my son Henry were at the Play, and my son John came in at half price. *Point of Honour* – new and *Don Juan*.

16th May.

Went to the Play at half price and sat in the side box. *Pizarro* and *No Song No Supper*.

27th May.

Benefit of Mr. and Mrs. Wright – *Poor Gentleman* and *Fortune's Frolick*.

8th June.

. . . at the Play – *Marriage Promise* – new – and *Magic Oak* a Pantomime[68] new –. It was the fullest house I think I ever saw. We got into the Playhouse with the greatest difficulty but I got a good seat. They took I heard 43 Pounds and turned away near 20.

17th June.

. . . for benefit of Mr. Butler, *John Bull*[69] and – both new. We were all very well entertained. There was a very full house indeed. Last night of acting this season.

There is no further information until the Whitby season of 1803-4 but sometime in 1803 an important event for the company's future took place; Mrs. Butler gave birth to her son Samuel.[70]

The Whitby theatre at its opening on 16th November is described as newly painted and with new scenery. On the opening night Meadows spoke 'An occasional, comic, nautical Address (in character of a Lieutenant)'[71] which is of interest as it includes a mention of the company's orchestra. Immediately after the last subscription night on 26th December, two bespeaks were given, one by desire of the Ladies and Gentlemen of the

Assembly, the other by desire of Capt. Preston and Officers of the Loyal Sea Fencibles; later two more were held for the Freemasons and for Capt. Simpson and the Loyal Whitby Volunteers. The benefits started on 2nd January and the last was for Butler himself on 10th February. The usual range of pieces was presented: 24 comedies, 12 musical farces, 9 farces, 7 comic operas, 5 melodramas, 4 tragedies, 3 plays, 2 pantomimes and 1 opera. Colman the Younger contributed 9 pieces, O'Keeffe 7 and Shakespeare 4 (*King John, Henry IV, Romeo and Juliet* and *Richard III*). An interesting revival was that of the Dryden-Purcell opera *King Arthur*. Plays new to London in 1803 were Dimond's *Hero of the North,* Colman the Younger's *John Bull* and *Love Laughs at Locksmiths,* Allingham's *Marriage Promise,* Holcroft's *Hear Both Sides,* Cobb's *Wife of Two Husbands,* Kenny's *Raising the Wind;* new to London in 1802 were Thomas Dibdin's *Cabinet,* Boaden's *Voice of Nature,* Holcroft's *Tale of Mystery,* Oulton's *Sixty-Third Letter,* Reynolds's *Delays and Blunders,* Cobb's *House to be Sold.* Of the local plays *The Fall of Carthage* was not repeated but *Streanstall Abbey* was given a performance for the third succeeding season. A large number of fresh performers had joined the company: Smith, Stuart, W. Stuart, Dunning, Clifton, Stannard, Worrall and Miss Ward. Fawcett, Fenton, Webber, Meggett and Murray are no longer mentioned nor does Wright appear though Mrs. Wright continued with the company until 1806. Thus of the family of the first Mrs. Butler none now was left, Wallises, Tayleures and Wright had all departed. John Courtney saw the players in Beverley on 14th June 1804, at an evening by the desire of the Race Stewards Sir Mark Sykes and Joseph Thomson, but he does not tell us the plays that were performed.

One playbill for the Harrogate season in 1804 records the performance of Allingham's new comedy *The Marriage Promise* on 14th August for the benefit of Jefferson and Miss Wood. Miss Wood was later in the year to become Mrs. George Jefferson under amusing circumstances. They are narrated by the Rev. James Tate in a letter to Eliza Wallis dated at Richmond 9th September:

> Mr. Jefferson, the Romeo of our stage, would fain be married to a lisping Juliet, Miss Wood; and has held deep consultation with me last night and this morning, how the feat is to be achieved in the face of the law. They have only resided here a week, and a licence cannot be had, except one of the parties has resided a month in the place. Then they are engaged with the manager of the Dumfries company, and wished to set off or take their exit O.P. on Tuesday morning for Penrith in the character of Mr. and Mrs. Jefferson. And what is to be done, if they cannot get up the part in due time? Marry, I know not, except to marry – at the fortnight end – in the land of lakes.

The winter of 1804 saw the company at Ulverston from 1st November to 29th December. Eighteen plays were given during these two months, including five classics: *King Lear, The Provok'd Husband, She Stoops to Conquer, Pizarro* and *George Barnwell.* Ulverston was given the opportunity of seeing several of London's recent successes: Boaden's *Voice of Nature* (1802), T. J. Dibdin's *English Fleet in 1342* (1803), Cobb's *Wife of Two Husbands* (1803), Dimond's *Hero of the North,* Allingham's *Marriage Promise* and two comedies which had appeared only in 1804, Cherry's *Soldier's Daughter* and Cumberland's *Sailor's Daughter.*

In 1805 George Ashburner published at Ulverston a slim volume entitled:

Thespian Gleanings, A Collection of Comic Recitals, Songs, Tales &c. Selected and Adapted from Foote – George Alexander – Stevens – O'Keeffe – Dibdin – Colman – Gibson – G. S. Carey – T. Dibdin, Cross – Dodd, Harrison – C. Dibdin &c. &c. – and many originals by T. Meadows, Comedian.[73]

The book is dedicated by Tom Meadows to Samuel Butler:

. . . as a small tribute of respect, to the members and visitors of the society of strangers at home, or theatrical club; to every son of Thespis and to a candid public'

The dedication is dated from the Theatre, Ulverston, 28th December 1804. The selection was collected at various times to serve for benefits and was published at the particular request of several friends. It includes many pieces in verse and prose, sung or recited by members of the company at the various circuit theatres, topical, humorous and narrative. Those which were heard at Richmond were '*The United Englishmen* or *Every Man a Volunteer,* Sung by Mr. Meadows, Theatres, Richmond, Whitby, Ripon. &c.'; '*Captain Wattle and Miss Roe* (Dibdin) sung by Mr. Davis, Theatres, Richmond and Whitby' and '*Billy Whipstitch; The Tailor's Ramble* as recited by M. Meadows, Theatre, Richmond.' Two pieces had been recited by Master Meadows: *The Orphan Boy's Tale; or Battle of the Nile* at Beverley and A Comic, Poetic, Heroic, Loyal Address in the character of Tom Thumb at Kendal. The *Origin of Old Bachelors* had been sung by Jefferson at Beverley, and the *Country Club* (Dibdin) at Harrogate by Butler. Although most of the pieces were those sung or recited by Meadows himself, Wright, Dunning, Davis, Bennett are also mentioned as having delivered some. Indeed the selection gives a very fair idea of the kind of interlude that was performed between the play and the farce.

After quitting Ulverston Butler spent the early spring in Kendal. A bill[74] for 1st April 1805 there gives *Henry VIII* with the following cast: King Henry – Clifton, Wolsey – Butler, Cranmer – Smith, D. of Norfolk – Davis, D. of Buckingham – Calcote, E. of Surrey – Darley, Ld. Chamberlain –

Stuart, Capucius – Martin, Sands – Meadows, Sir Thos. Lovell – Dunning, Cromwell – Neville, Surveyor – George, Queen Katherine – Mrs. Butler, Anne Bullen – Mrs. Fenton, Old Lady – Mrs. Fildew, Duchess of Norfolk – Mrs. Darley, Marchioness of Dorset – Mrs. Martin, Patience – Mrs. Murray, Countess of Suffolk – Miss Jefferson. The advertised attractions of the piece were a grand banquet and dance, the trial of Queen Katharine in Act II, and the christening of Queen Elizabeth in Act V. This was followed, for the last time that season, by the pantomime *Cinderella:*

With the original Music, new Scenery, Machinery &c. The Scenery painted by Mr. Stuart and Mr. Dunning, dresses and Decorations by Mrs. Murray and Mrs. Fildew.

The effects were listed as follows:

The Rosy Bower of Venus. Cupids flying in the Air, In different attitudes, with Wreaths of Roses &c. Venus reclined on a Bank of Roses, Attended by the Graces. A Pedestal and figure of Cinderella. The Pedestal becomes a most magnificent Coach, And the figure of Cinderella is transformed to Diana the Huntress. Cinderella's Kitchen, With a Dresser and Pumpkin. The Fairy and Cupid disguis'd as Beggars. The Pumpkin and Dresser changed to a most magnificent State Chariot, drawn by Cupids. The Ball Room. The Star of Venus is seen crossing the Stage. The Hall of Audience Where Cinderella tries on the Glass Slipper. The Brilliant Temple of Venus. The whole to conclude with the Marriage of the Prince and Cinderella.

This was a chance for the children of the company and Masters Meadows, H. Meadows, Holliday, Darley, Wright and Butler and Miss Butler all appeared. This is the first we hear of the Butler children on the stage; Miss Butler was about five and Samuel only two years old.

Calcote, Neville and Mrs. Fenton were new players but all had left by the end of the year.

The last of Butler's new theatres, that at Beverley was opened on Monday, 13th May 1805.[75] The previous building in Walkergate had become too small and incommodious[76] and the new theatre was erected in Lairgate by a mason named Thomas Leck at the expense of Abraham Peacock a druggist of the town. It seated 632 and possessed neat boxes, a pit and a gallery. A bust of Shakespeare was placed over the centre of the stage.[77]

Two Harrogate bills in the British Library for 1805 record a performance on 6th August for the benefit of Mrs. Butler at which she played Lady Teazle to her husband's Sir Peter, and also a production of Tobin's new comedy *The Honeymoon* with entirely new dresses on 8th August. During the Whitby season of 1805-6 Butler catered for the enthusiasm for child prodigies, aroused by the performances of the Young

Roscius, Master Betty, by engaging Master Williams, the Young Roscius of York, to play with the company for two nights. He took the part of Douglas to Butler's Lord Randolph in Home's tragedy, and Fred in the Kotzebue-Inchbald *Lovers' Vows*. Butler also engaged Saxoni the rope dancer to exhibit his surprising feats on the tight rope for a few performances at the end of the season. The Freemasons had a bespeak when:

> Between the play and the farce a regular Free Masons Lodge will be formed on the stage when the Brethren will appear in their Proper Dresses according to their different orders and Masonic Toasts and songs sung by the Brothers of the Lodge.

This season the company presented 22 comedies, 10 musical farces, 9 melodramas, 7 tragedies, 7 farces, 5 comic operas, 2 plays, 1 interlude, 1 ballad opera and 1 pantomime. Of these 6 pieces were by Thomas Dibdin and 5 by Colman the Younger, 4 by Shakespeare (*Lear* with Mrs. Butler as Cordelia, *As You Like It, Romeo and Juliet, Henry VIII*), and 4 by Reynolds. An otherwise unknown piece by Stephen Kemble entitled *Coal Trade or Adventures in a Coal Pit!!!* was brought out on 14th February.

Plays new to London in 1805 were Tobin's *Honeymoon*, Reynolds's *Out of Place*, Mrs. Inchbald's *To Marry or Not to Marry*, Morton's *School of Reform*, Miss Chambers's *School for Friends;* new to London in 1804 were *Cinderella*, Thomas Dibdin's *Thirty Thousand, Will for the Deed* and *Valentine and Orson (As the Brazen Oracle)*, Kenney's *Matrimony*, Dimond's *Hunter of the Alps*, Cumberland's *Sailor's Daughter*, Cherry's *Soldier's Daughter*, Hoare's *Paragraph* and Reynolds's *Blind Bargain*. Ryder, Scruton, Watson and Mrs. Dunning are new names. The two Butler children appeared in Morton's *Children in the Wood*.

When the company went on to Ripon, Mrs. Butler's father Thomas Jefferson, now an old man, returned to his native town and there the young Meadows remembered him 'a feeble old man sitting by the fireside ill with gout, and tended by one of his daughters; and there on 24th January 1807 he died.'[78] When the company were at Northallerton in the spring of 1806 they were joined by a young man of 17 named Carey from Moss's company in Dumfries.[79] He was none other than Edmund Kean and he 'did the walking gentleman, harlequin, and comic singing for 15s. a week.'[80] He is said to have shared a truckle bed with the old actor George who foresaw his brilliant promise. According to Hawkins it was when he appeared for the first time as Octavian in *The Mountaineers*, that he attracted the attention of a gentleman connected with the Haymarket who undertook to secure him an engagement there if he could reach London within a specified time. He succeeded in doing this through the generosity of Butler who defrayed the expenses of a stage coach and was thus instrumental in launching the great actor on his London career. Kean did not forget as we shall see. He could only have been a month or two with the company at most as the Haymarket season started in June. His wage of 15/- was a usual one in the company for Donaldson tells us that Butler conducted the circuit:

> . . . with such success that he was always ready on the Saturday to meet his performers with their salaries, which were not very heavy – 15s. a week being the average; it was in fact a standing rule never to exceed that sum. No matter what talent an actor possessed, he must fall into the ranks like a common soldier, and be content with the common lot.

This rather unusual system seems to have worked well, the company flourished and actors enjoyed a measure of security which it was not easy to obtain in the provinces.

There were two seasons at Harrogate in 1806 for which I have a number of playbills. The first is dated 14th May but is not the first one of the season, the last is for Tuesday, 16th September which was in the last week of the players' visit. In between these two dates the company was at Beverley where Stephen Kemble played with them for three nights in July as Falstaff and Job Thornberry.[81] During his visits to Harrogate Butler contrived to enlist the services of five notable visitors. There was first the rope dancer Saxoni the last night of whose engagement was announced on 14th May. In addition to the usual feats on the tight rope Saxoni:

> . . . presented a Variety of curious and interesting Hydraulic Experiments – Mr. Saxoni will produce several curious Effects, on an entire new plan, which have never been exhibited in Public by any Person. – They consist of A Globe, from which Water is produced in a Variety of Shapes. This Apparatus may be placed in a Room, Garden, or carried about, and producing all the Effects without the aid of Human Power.

The theatre of these days had room for every kind of entertainment and experiment and was at once a playhouse, music hall, circus and palace of wonders. In July Stephen Kemble came on with the company from Beverley for two nights. On 10th July he acted Job Thornberry in *John Bull* and on 15th July Penruddock in *The Wheel of Fortune*. The inevitable child prodigy was the next attraction. On 19th July there appeared:

> Miss Ferron for one night only. – Mr. Butler presents his respects to the Ladies and Gentlemen at Harrogate, has the pleasure to inform them he has engaged Miss Ferron from London, a Musical Wonder, only Ten years old, with such a compass of Voice never heard in England before.

She and Mr. Cobham gave a Musical Entertainment between the play and the farce 'Consisting of some of the most favourite Songs, and Instrumental Pieces, as performed at York, with the most Rapturous Applause.' Lastly came a more famous singer; on 24th July Incledon performed with Bartley and Horn from Drury Lane 'On their Road to Edinborough.' Incledon played Captain Campley in *Inkle and Yarico* with additional songs to Bartley's Inkle. In the interval he sang two songs and a duet with Horn, composed for them by Shield and then performed Steady in *The Quaker* with Bartley as Sloman and Horn as Lubin. On 14th August there was a benefit for Melvin who had been temporarily engaged by the company. Harrogate, lying on the route from London to Edinburgh, Butler was able to entice men such as Incledon to play there on their way to their engagements in Scotland.

Among the plays new to Harrogate during this season were Thomas Dibdin's *Valentine and Orson*, and *Thirty Thousand*, Dimond's *Hunter of the Alps*, Miss Chambers's *School for Friends* (these had been given by the company at Whitby), Allingham's *Weathercock*, Colman the Younger's *We Fly By Night*, Cherry's *Travellers* and Hook's *Invisible Girl*, the last three produced in London that year. There was also 'an entire new Pantomime called *Mother Shipton or Harlequin in Knaresborough*' which came out on 16th September and obviously catered for local interest (this may be a version of the pantomime of *Mother Shipton*, with music by S. Arnold, produced at Covent Garden in 1770). It was provided 'With new Scenery & Machinery, Painted by Mr. Dunning – A View of the Well House which changes to The Dropping Well', and included 'The celebrated Dying Scene of Harlequin. And the Skeleton Scene from Doctor Faustus.'

Dunning was at this time the company's scene painter, as well as actor and dancer. New scenery, machinery and dresses were also provided for *Valentine and Orson* including 'a View of the inside of King Pepin's Palace.' 'A new scene appropriate to the Piece' was painted for *Thirty Thousand*:
> . . . consisting of the following designs. viz: A Horse Race – Two Misers – A Sea Fight – The Spartan Thief – A Black Boy – An Old Woman Frying Fritters by Fire-light – A Doctor's Shop – The Story of Le Fevre and The Head of a great Actor.

The habit of giving a synopsis, comparable to a film trailer, especially of new melodramas, was growing on the playbills. Thus one's appetite for *Valentine and Orson* was whetted by an outline of the plot. Plays were more often given a puff from the moral point of view. Thus after a few lines concerning the main plot of *King Lear* comes the tag:
> . . . the justice of Providence in the punishment of the Guilty, and rewarding the virtuous, are circumstances which inspire to please, astonish and instruct.

King Lear, in Tate's version of course, was cast as follows: Lear – Butler, Gloster – Smith, Kent – Meadows, Bastard – Ryder, Cornwall – Watson, Albany – Darley, Burgundy – Dunning, Gentleman Usher – Davis, Old Man – George, Edgar – Jefferson, Captain – Bywater, Officers – Messrs.

Martin and Worrall, Goneril – Mrs. Murray, Regan – Mrs. Jefferson, Arante – Miss Jefferson, Cordelia – Miss Butler.

In *As You Like It* the dramatis personae were: Duke – Ryder, Duke Frederick – Martin, Jacques – Butler, Amiens – Watson, Le Beau – George, Oliver – Darley, Orlando – Jefferson, Adam – Smith, Corin – Meadows, Touchstone – Davis, Silvius – Dunning, Charles – Worrall, Rosalind – Mrs. Darley, Celia – Mrs. Murray, Phoebe – Mrs. Jefferson, Audrey – Miss Jefferson. Thus some idea may be obtained of the type of parts allotted to the various members of the company. Master and Miss Butler again appeared in *The Children in the Wood* and Master Meadows recited and Master H. Meadows danced one evening between play and afterpiece. New names are Thompson and Bywater who made his first appearance on 7th August. Besides the actors there were attached to the company for many years Kelly and Thomas and William Mercer; William was leader of the band but we do not know what Thomas did; there was also a Stage Keeper.

In addition to bespeaks by private people it was the habit of the leading hotels in Harrogate to bespeak evenings. Thus we have 'By desire of the Ladies and Gentlemen at the Granby' and another for those at The Dragon. Tickets, for all occasions except benefits, were handled by Hargrove's Library as well as by Butler at the theatre, and the printing was done by John Martin. Lord Byron visited the theatre this season in the company of Professor Hailstone but has unfortunately left us no record of his impressions.[82] The theatre is henceforward described as a Theatre Royal.

We have a glimpse of the company at Richmond in an entry, under the date 2nd October, from a book at Lennox Lodge, recording that John Martin Painter, and John Martin Stallkeeper both of Butler's company were visitors there. John Martin painter was presumably the same John Martin who printed the playbills at Harrogate where the theatre seems to have possessed a printing press. We know too that a John Martin was prompter in the company. One wonders if John Martin stallkeeper looked after the horse or horses which drew the wagon on which the scenery and properties were conveyed from one town to the other.

Stephen Kemble joined the company in Ulverston and for his benefit on 10th January performed Falstaff in *The Merry Wives* and delivered 'A Cento' from the works of Shakespeare addressed to the Volunteers of the United Kingdom.

The Ulverston season lasted from 6th November to 10th January.[83] In addition to *The Merry Wives*, three other Shakespeare plays were performed: *Richard III*, *Othello* and *Henry IV*. Only *George Barnwell* survived from the previous season but nine new pieces were added to the repertory. Of these three dated from 1805, Mrs. Inchbald's *To Marry or Not to Marry*, Tobin's *Honeymoon*, and Colman's *Who Wants a Guinea?* and

Cherry's *Travellers* from 1806. The company went on to Kendal where they stayed for the long period of three months.

A set of bills for the winter season there in 1807 is in possession of the Kendal Museum. The first bill dated 14th January and the last night was on Friday, 17th April. Playing evenings were Mondays, Wednesdays and Fridays, performances started at seven, and charges were the usual ones of boxes 3/-, pit 2/-, gallery 1/-. Stephen Kemble came from Ulverston to play for three nights and opened on 12th January as Falstaff in *Henry IV* with Jefferson as Prince of Wales and Mrs. Murray as Lady Percy.[83a] On Wednesday, 14th January he acted Penruddock. He evidently performed also on Friday 16th though there is no bill for this date, but on Monday 19th it was announced that he had offered to perform again that evening, which would be positively his last night. For this occasion he chose the role of Thornberry in *John Bull* to Butler's Dennis Brulgruddery.

A number of new plays and afterpieces were given including Dimond's *Hunter of the Alps* and *Adrian and Orrila*, Kenney's *Matrimony*, Mrs. Inchbald's *To Marry or Not to Marry*, Cherry's *Travellers*, Reynolds's *Out of Place*, Allingham's *Weathercock*, Tobin's *Honeymoon*, Thomas Dibdin's *Thirty Thousand*, Colman the Younger's *We Fly By Night* and *Who wants a Guinea?* and Hook's *Soldier's Return*. *The Travellers* and *Who wants a Guinea?* met with such applause that they were repeated. Some interesting details are given about the setting of these and other pieces. *The Travellers* was put on:

> With new Scenery, Machinery, Dresses, &c. The Scenery by Mr. Dunning, the Dresses by Mrs. Murray, Mrs. Fildew, and Miss Jefferson. Scenery, A Chinese Garden, a Chinese Chamber, The Emperor's Throne, a Complete Deck of a British Man of War with a Mainmast, Rigging, Guns &c. &c.

Out of Place had:

> Scenery and Machinery proper for the piece: particularly, the Castle and the Lake, which is destroyed by the Soldiers, and discovers Timothy, Young Valtelini and Lauretta, on a part of the Lake.

Paul and Virginia after staging the celebrations of Virginia's birthday and the natives ornamenting her cottage with wreaths of flowers concluded with the popular shipwreck scene:

> . . . a tremendous Storm. – a Ship in Distress is struck by Lightening, sinks – Virginia is seen floating in the Waves. – Paul jumps from a Rock into the Sea. Alambra puts off a Boat to save Virginia – Virginia is brought on Shore by Paul and Alambra.

44

The pantomime *Magic Oak or Harlequin Triumphant* was produced:

> With new Scenery, Dresses, Music, Machinery, Magical Deceptions, and Pantomimical Devices. The Principal Scenes are the Cave of Merlin, with the Magic Oak withered – a beautiful Grotto of Shell Work – a wonderful Deception with a magical Chest – a Wind-Mill – The Magic Oak in full Leaf – Superb Golden Statue of Marcus Aurelius in the Capitol of Rome (as Large as Life) – a ludicrous Metamorphose from the Change of a Table – a Prison – and a beautiful Bower, with Garlands of Roses; in the Centre, a Fountain in Motion, with Figures spouting Water &c. &c.

Dunning performed Harlequin 'with a variety of Leaps'. Scenery for scenery's sake was also indulged in and Dunning designed and executed for display:

> A Grand Emblematical Transparent Painting – Representing the Figures of Britannia, Neptune and Fame, With other emblematical Devices, And a beautiful Medallion (as Large as Life) of Lord Nelson.

When *The Castle Spectre* was presented Butler assured 'his Friends, and the Public, that he has not spared any Expense to render it worthy their Approbation and Support.' For the last four nights Butler, after expressing himself 'ever anxious to contribute to the entertainment of the Ladies and Gentlemen of Kendal, and the Public in general,' announced the engagement of Saxoni the tight-rope dancer.

Of the actors Beverley from Leicester and Norwich, Clifton and Watson from York, Miss Craven from Norwich and Miss Davis were new. Miss Craven became one of the company's leading ladies and was with them ten years. Master and Miss Butler were Cupids in *Cinderella* and were reinforced by the children of the town; they also played the children in *The Stranger* to which Master Butler added Fernando in *Pizarro*. Master Meadows spoke a new occasional address 'Being his last appearance on any Stage', though he was playing again the next winter! A rather puzzling matter is the deletion in a Ms. hand of many names and the substitution of Finn, G. Butler, Smithson, Mrs. Felix and the Wilsons. The Wilsons made their first appearance in Whitby in 1809-10 and were not in the company at this time, the others were all in the company for the Whitby season of 1807-8. One can only surmise that these were changes that took place in casts during the 1809 season at Kendal. Of greater interest is the Ms. addition of receipts taken at each benefit. since these give some indication of the popularity of plays and players I have tabulated them in the order of amount of receipts.

45

Date	Benefit	Plays	Receipts
10th Apr.	Miss Jefferson, Miss Craven, Beverley, (2nd benefit, 1st failed owing to inclement weather, See Mar. 16)	*Who Wants a Guinea? Maid of the Oaks*, Saxoni on tight rope	£78.4.0.
23rd Feb.	Clifton	*Stranger, Fortune's Frolic*	55.5.6.
11th Mar.	Mr. & Mrs. Davis	*Battle of Hexham, Gretna Green*	54.3.0.
6th Mar.	Meadows (ms. Mrs. Butler)	*Jealous Wife, No Song No Supper*	34.8.6.
30th Mar.	Mrs. Butler	*Adrian and Orrila, Out of Place*	33.6.0.
Easter Monday 21st Mar.	Mr. & Mrs. Martin	*Dramatist, Waterman*	27.15.0.
20th Mar.	Watson	*Rivals, Inkle & Yarico*	27.1.0.
1st Apr.	Mrs. Fildew (ms. Mr. & Mrs. Wilson, Smithson)	*School for Scandal*	27.1.0.
8th Apr.	Mrs. Meadows, W. & T. Mercer, Kelly, Worrall, J. Martin	*Blind Bargain, Irishman in London*	24.15.6.
27th Feb.	Mr. & Mrs. Dunning	*Poor Gentleman, We Fly By Night*	22.15.0.
13th Mar.	Jefferson	*Way to Get Married, Highland Reel*	22.2.0.
4th Mar.	George, Mrs. Murray	*Speed the Plough, Love Laughs at Locksmiths*	21.14.0.
3rd Apr.	Mrs. Jefferson	*Soldier's Daughter, Weathercock*	20.12.0.
16th Mar.	Miss Jefferson (cf. 10th Apr.)	*Wife of Two Husbands, Soldier's Return*	13.9.6.

It was the rope dancer who brought the very large amount of £78.4.0. Miss Jefferson's £13.9.6. was considered a failure and she was allowed the share of another benefit. The average of these receipts is £36 but this is probably above what an actor might expect as there can be little doubt that the £78, which brings up the average, was but rarely netted.

A playbill for Harrogate dated 4th August 1807 gives *Lovers' Vows* and *The Sultan*:

Mr. Butler has the pleasure to announce that A LADY for amusement, on THIS NIGHT ONLY and for the FIRST TIME of her ever performing, will undertake the Characters of Amelia Wildenhaim, in the Play & Roxalana, in the Farce.

a ms. hand has added that the lady was Mrs. Foote. In between the comedy and the farce one Atkins danced a military hornpipe in which he was advertised to go:

. . . through part of the MANUAL and PLATOON EXERCISE, and Fire off the Gun, fixed to his Forehead.

The next information we have about the company is for the following winter season at Whitby in 1807-8. The season ran from 19th November to 19th February and the subscription was for 21 nights. Twenty-three comedies, 11 farces, 10 musical farces, 8 tragedies, 7 comic operas, 7 melodramas, 4 pantomimes, 3 plays and 1 operatic romance were given. Of these 8 were by Colman the Younger, 6 by Shakespeare (*Othello, Romeo and Juliet, Merchant of Venice, Richard III, Hamlet* and *Macbeth*) and 6 by Thomas Dibdin. Beaumont and Fletcher's *Rule a Wife and Have a Wife* was revived by the company after 25 years. An otherwise unknown comic drama was called *The Reformation or What We All Want* 'in which will be introduced the laughable story and adventures of three celebrated thieves' was produced on 8th February 1808. It was written, together with its prologue and epilogue, by Mrs. Felix, an actress in the company. Productions new to London in 1807 were Cherry's *Peter the Great*, Morton's *Town and Country*, Tobin's *Curfew*, Siddons's *Time's a Tell Tale*, this last being presented at a benefit for Mrs. Butler by desire of the ladies of Whitby; new to London in 1806 were Colman the Younger's *We Fly By Night* and *The Forty Thieves*, Dimond's *Adrian and Orrila*, Cherry's *Travellers*, Hook's *Invisible Girl*, Thomas Dibdin's *Harlequin and Mother Goose* and *Five Miles Off*. New players who had joined the company were: Finn from New York, George Butler, Mrs. Brennan from Liverpool and Mrs. Felix who played just for the season and was announced on her first appearance as 'A Lady, who played with great success at Harrogate, and on whom Mr. Butler has prevailed to act in Whitby.' George Butler was with the company until 1811. In June the company was in Beverley where they gave Kenney's melodrama *The Blind Boy* for which Dunning had prepared new scenery including 'a Magnificent Temple, Rocks and a Terrace illuminated with lamps.' Bannister then played for one night on 29th June as Shiva (*The Jew*) and in Hoare's *The Prize*.[84]

In 1808 the company wintered at Ulverston from 27th October to 31st December.[85] *The Merchant of Venice* and *Macbeth* were the two Shakespeare plays given and *She Stoops to Conquer* and Mrs. Centlivre's *The Wonder* were also revived. An otherwise unknown version of the pantomime *Mother Goose* was among the attractions. Two of Cumberland's plays, *The Fashionable Lover* (1772) and *The Jew* (1794) were revived as well as Reynolds's *The Dramatist* (1781) and Thompson's *The Stranger* (1798). Two plays dated from 1807: H. Siddons's *Time's a Tell Tale* and the ever-popular Cherry's, *Peter the Great*. Reynolds's *Begone Dull Care* had had its premiere only in February 1808 presumably the company then progressed to Kendal as was its wont.

A single playbill for the Harrogate season of 1809 dated 5th September records that Fawcett from Covent Garden played for this night only, and took the roles of Ollapod in Colman the Younger's *Poor Gentleman* and Lingo in O'Keeffe's *Agreeable Surprise*.

Butler's twenty-one year lease of the Richmond Theatre expired in May 1809 but as far back as 24th September 1801 he had been granted an additional term of ten years to commence from May 1809 at an increased rent of £10 under the same covenants and restrictions as were contained in his former lease.[86] On 10th October the Rev. James Tate records a Richmond School bespeak of Tobin's *Honeymoon* and Ravenscroft's *Anatomist*, the house being about £30.

The Whitby season opened on 22nd November with a subscription of 21 nights and closed on 23rd February. Butler was ill during part of the season and the production of Reynolds's *Begone Dull Care* was postponed on 26th December. 'On account of Mr. Butler being very much indisposed.' The company presented 24 comedies, 12 tragedies, 10 melodramas, 9 farces, 9 operatic farces, 5 comic operas, 4 plays, 1 opera, 1 operatic romance and 1 pantomime. Nine of Colman's plays, 7 of Shakespeare's, 5 of Kenney's and 4 of Dimond's were given. It was therefore a particularly good season for Shakespeare. The plays presented were *Hamlet* with Finn as Hamlet, Butler as the Ghost and G. Butler as Guildenstern, *Macbeth* with Finn as Macbeth, *Merchant of Venice, Romeo and Juliet, Richard III, Othello* and *King Lear*. To have put on the four major tragedies in one season was not a bad effort for a provincial company. The two Whitby plays were also revived this winter Gibson's *Streanstall Abbey* on 18th December and Watkins's *Fall of Carthage* on 3rd January. New Members of the company were Mr. and Mrs. Wilson from Edinburgh, Hallam from Sheffield, Taylor and Stoker.

I said in the first chapter that one of the respects in which we were singularly lucky in dealing with this circuit was the existence of a practically complete series of playbills of the company from 1st March 1810 to 11th March 1811. They are in the possession of Mr. Ewan Kerr of Kendal who most generously sent them to me to examine. They carry on the story of the company's activities from the time of their leaving Whitby in 1810.

We are thus enabled to trace the itinerary which led the company from a centre in Ripon across east to Beverley and back centre to Harrogate; from there north to Richmond and Northallerton and thence across to Ulverston and Kendal. The distances along what must have been many rough roads were great and four to six days were generally allowed between stations. Stays averaged about two months. Over a two year period the company's circuit took them almost across the country from Whitby on the east coast to Kendal in the Lake District and Ulverston in the Furness peninsula. Of course, Butler never played in the same winter season both east and west but alternated between Whitby and the two Cumbrian towns. The distances travelled bear witness to the scarcity of rival companies operating in the region though in 1811 King, a circuit manager from the north penetrated to the rather isolated Furness peninsula.

Butler opened at the Theatre Royal, Ripon, on 1st March and acted there on Tuesdays, Thursdays and Saturdays until 17th May, when a Benefit for Mrs. Butler closed the season. There was, of course, no playing during Passion Week but on Easter Monday there was a benefit for Butler instead of a Tuesday performance. The following bespoke evenings: Lady Grantham, Gentlemen Farmers, the Mayor and Corporation, Gentlemen of the Ripon Hunt, and the Masons of the Royal Oak Lodge. On this last occasion the players formed a Lodge on the stage and the masonic transparency was displayed. On 24th March, for four days, a tight rope performer named Richer was engaged and the following puff appeared on the playbills:

Mr. Butler respectfully announces, that ever anxious and un-remittingly studious to give all possible variety and addition to the entertainments of the Town and Neighbourhood, he has engaged for four Nights that inimitable Performer Mr. Richer, whose unequalled elegance and unparalleled Exhibitions on the Tight Rope, have gained him the sanction and applause of the first Courts on the Continent, as well as the Patronage of the Royal Family of England: Richer's Performances at the Theatres-Royal, Bath, Dublin, Edinburgh, York, &c. &c. &c. have drawn full and fashionable Audiences every Year since his first Appearance.

A claim is even made that he is established in public opinion 'as The First Rope-Dancer in Europe.' His performances varied every evening and nothing under full price was taken during his stay. He concluded his visit with a benefit. Another kind of playbill puff is that to *Venice Preserv'd*:

> The loves and distresses of Jaffier and Belvidera, must, call forth the applauding tear: In the character of Pierre, real courage is depicted in such language, that the most rigid must admire it, though executed in the cause of rebellion.

As usual local interest was encouraged. On one evening George spoke an occasional address to the ladies and gentlemen of Ripon, on another Mr. Joseph Barker of Bondgate contributed a comic song, on a third a hornpipe was danced by a local youth, on a fourth a young lady of Ripon made her first appearance on any stage and sang a song. At the end of his season in every town Butler paid his humble respects to his patrons, thanked them for the favours conferred on him and assured them that he would make it his study to merit their future support. This attitude of humility and gratitude was expected and a manager who refused to express it duly suffered.

Plays new to Ripon were Hoare's *Three and the Deuce*, Colman the Younger's *Africans*, Hook's *Tekeli* and *Killing No Murder*, Reynolds's *Exile* and *Free Knights*, Leigh's *Grieving's a Folly* and Dimond's *Foundling of the Forest*. *Tekeli* was so popular that after two performances Butler was desired to give a third because so many people had been disappointed of seeing it.

A good many of the new plays were provided with new scenery by Dunning. Descriptions of these new scenes are often given at length and are interesting as showing the company's resources and technique. Melodrama particularly called for frequent scene changes and marvellous effects. Here is what was attempted for Kenney's *Blind Boy*:

> The Farm-Yard of Oberto, and a Rustic Bridge over which the Prince and Hunters (from the Chace) visit the cottage of the Blind Boy. Procession to the Palace of Stanislaus, to celebrate the nuptials of Prince Rodolph and Lida, View from the Banks of the Vistula. – A Terrace Fronting a stupendous Rock, where a Battle takes place between Kalig and Starow, during a Thunder Storm, the defeat of Starow who is thrown into the Sea by Kalig, the Protector of the Royal Orphan.

The Africans was supplied with:

> . . . new Scenery, Dresses and other African Decorations; the Scenery Painted by Mr. Dunning – Act the First, – A Negro Bridal Dance, Scenery. 1st – A View of the Town of Fatteconda in Bondon, A District of Africa inhabited by the Foulahs, and situated between the Rivers Senegal and Gambia. 2nd – The Interior of Ferulho's House. 3rd – Ferulho's Tent, with a distant View of the Town of Fatteconda. 4th – The Town of Fatteconda in Ruins. 5th – The Camp of the Mandingo King.

Supers specially engaged for the occasion played the negro slaves. The topographical element was much to the fore in scene design at this period and various views of localities are of frequent occurrence in scene plots. Take the scenery painted by Dunning for *Tekeli*:

The Interior of the Mill of Keben through which is seen a Perspective View of the Fortress of Mongatz. With part of the River, Bridge, Water-Mill, Wind-Mill, &c. Ancient Hall within the Fortress of Mongatz. Interior Battlements – Arrival of Tekeli – Entire View of The Walls, Towers and Bastions – The Siege!!! Springing of the Mine – Destruction of the Battlements – The Austrians succeed in making a Breach. Fall of Caraffa. Mongatz on Fire. Standards taken by Alexina and the Victory of Tekeli.

For *The Exile* Dunning painted 'An extensive Country in Siberia, cover'd with Snow, Rocky view and the Town of Tobolskow, with the River Wolga.' The effects included 'The Coronation of the Empress Elizabeth, a Masquerade and Dance.' Rock sets were frequently used. Dunning's scenery for *Free Knights* was:

A Spacious Cavern, with a new set of Rock Wings, and Brazen Door, where the Free Knights kept their Prisoners and held their Court, – A View of Corbey Abbey, a Chateau, the Gates of Corbey, a splendid Gothic Hall, the statue of Charlemagne, the inside of Corbey Abbey with Banners of the Free Knights, Inscriptions, &c. &c.

The cavern and the brazen door came in handy for the scenery of *The Forty Thieves* which was as follows:

The Splendid Palace of the Fairy of the Lake – The Fairy Enters in her Chariot drawn by Sylphs, Gnomes and Naiads – The Road leading to the Wood – the Wood-Cutter's Cottage – The Wood and enchanted Cavern, with the Brazen Gates, where the Thieves conceal their Plunder – Orcobrand's Cave – A Street in Bagdad – The Gallery in Ali Baba's House, with the Forty Jars, which the Forty Thieves are concealed in to Murder the Family – The Grand Turkish Banquet – The Grotto of the Fairy – A Silver Lake on which are Swans Swimming.

Cherry's *Peter the Great* was enhanced by a scene representing a Dockyard, and among the advertised attractions of *Venice Preserv'd* was the exhibition of 'A Scaffold, cover'd with black, surmounted by Racks, Wheels, Chairs, and all the frightful instruments of Death.' People then as now enjoyed the contemplation of horrors.

Dunning was not only scene painter and actor but also acrobat. On one occasion he spoke Dr. Goldsmith's *Epilogue*, in character of Harlequin '. . . in the course of which he will take a Flying leap Through A Circle of Fixed Daggers.' Among the songs, dances and recitations that graced the interval between play and afterpiece may be remarked the recitation by Miss Stoker of Wordsworth's *Goody Blake and Harry Gill*.

Whilst the company was staying at Ripon the Richmond Theatre opened at least for one night. Timothy Hutton of Clifton who was at Richmond training with the local militia records in his ms. Diary under Friday, 11th May 1810: 'Went to the Theatre to hear Mrs. Inchbauld.' This was probably Mrs. George Inchbald who had been a member of the company in 1796. What kind of performance it was we cannot tell from Hutton's bald note; probably one of those one person entertainments by which players often supplemented their meagre earnings.[87]

On leaving Ripon the company went to Beverley opening there on 21st May and playing Mondays, Wednesdays and Fridays except during Race Week when they played every night but Tuesday and nothing under full price was taken. The season concluded on 5th July. Bespeaks were given by Col. Bethell and Officers of the 3rd East York local militia, by gentlemen of the Grammar School, by General Vyse, by the Stewards of the Races and by the Mayor and Corporation.

All the new plays given at Ripon except *The Exile* were repeated in Beverley and *Tekeli* again proved most popular and was accorded three performances.

Dunning's scenery and effects for the revival of Colman the Younger's *Blue Beard* and the effects were described as follows:

> In Act the First An Oriental Procession. Abomelique's Triumphal March to Demand the fair Fatima, attended by Janissaries, Spahis, Guards, Slaves, &c. In Act the Second, The Enchanted Blue Chamber, View of Blue Beard's Castle – and the Magic Sepulchre, which changes to a Brilliant Garden.

The transformation scene was thus exploited by melodrama as well as by pantomime.

Twice the evening concluded with *God Save the King* sung by Bennett with the rest of the company as chorus. Master Butler, now seven years old, played Charles Mortimer in Reynolds's *Laugh When You Can* and one of the children in *The Stranger*.

The Harrogate season opened on 10th July, five days after the closing of the Beverley one, and continued until 22nd September when Butler returned thanks to both Harrogate and Knaresborough patrons. Tuesday, Thursday and Saturday were playing nights. On 20th and 21st August the company returned for two nights to Ripon during the races there.

Harrogate was rich in bespeaks, 13 private individuals as well as two hotels (The Crown and the Queen's Head) desiring them. Many of these were given on benefit nights so that the actors whose benefit it was profited accordingly. The guest artist was Mrs. Charles Kemble who played for four nights at the beginning of September. On 4th September she played Bisarre in *The Inconstant* and Maria in *Of Age To-morrow;* on 5th September Letitia Hardy in *The Belle's Stratagem* and Edmond the Blind Boy in the melodrama of that name; on 6th September Mrs. Oakley in *The Jealous Wife* and Caroline in *The Prize*; the bill for the fourth occasion is missing. On 18th September *Richard III* was played by 'a Thespian from York' the rest of the cast being as follows: King Henry – Wilson, Duke of Buckingham – George, Prince Edward – Master Meadows, Duke of York – Master Butler, Tressel – Butler, Ld. Stanley – Martin, Catesby – G. Butler, Ld. Mayor – Davis, Ratcliffe – Dunning, Lieut. of the Tower – Smithson, Oxford – Hallam, E. of Richmond – a Gentleman 1st appearance on any stage, Lady Ann – Mrs. Murray, Duchess of York – Mrs. Martin, Queen – Mrs. Butler. The amateurs had to pay heavily for the privilege of acting with the professionals, but to give Butler his due he did not often indulge in this form of money-making.

On 31st July the pantomime of *Cinderella* again enlisted all the company's children for the flying Cupids, who were taken by Masters Butler, Jefferson, C. Jefferson and Dunning and Misses Davis and Wilson. Master Butler also performed *Tom Thumb*. His sister does not seem to have acted after 1807, until she re-appeared in 1813.

Six days after their last performance at Harrogate the company opened at Richmond on Friday, 28th September. The next bill for Monday, 1st October announces the last night until the races. After two performances they trekked to Northallerton where they spent a week from 2nd to 8th October acting every night but Sunday. On Tuesday, 9th October they re-opened at Richmond for race week and there are playbills for Wednesday 10th, Friday 12th, Saturday 13th, Monday 15th, Wednesday 17th, Friday 19th. I will deal with the short Richmond season as a whole, ignoring for the moment the interval at Northallerton. And first of all we may notice that the theatre, as all the theatres in Butler's circuit, had graduated to a Theatre Royal. The prices remained at the customary boxes 3/-, pit 2/-, gallery 1/- and performances began at 7 p.m. Tickets were to be had of Butler 'at Mr. Westgarths' and at the Theatre.' Playbills were printed by M. Craggs, M. Bell, Thomas Bowman, Smith and L. Macfarlane.

The season opened with *Venice Preserv'd* which had not been acted at Richmond for 30 years. The cast was as follows: Duke of Venice – Hallam, Priuli – Wilson, Bedamar – Smithson, Pierre – Butler, Jaffier – Bennett, Renault – George, Elliott – Davis, Spinosa – Dunning, Theodore – Martin, Captain of the Guard – G. Butler, Executioner – Stoker, Belvidera – Mrs. Butler. After some songs by George Butler and the versatile Dunning, Hook's farce *Killing No Murder* was brought out for the first time at Richmond with the following players: Sir Wm. Wilton – George, Jack

Wilton – Smithson, Appollo Belvie – Dunning, Buskin – Davis, Tap –
G. Butler, Mrs. Watchet – Mrs. Wilson, Miss Nancy – Mrs. Jefferson,
Fanny – Mrs. Dunning.

On 1st October the first production in Richmond of Leigh's comedy
Grieving's a Folly was followed by *The Forty Thieves* with the same scenery
as described in Ripon. On their return from Northallerton the company
opened on Tuesday, 9th October with *The Inconstant* with the following
cast: Old Mirabel – Davis, Young Mirabel – Jefferson, Capt. Duretete –
Butler, Dugard – Smithson, Petit – Dunning, Page – Master Butler, Bravos
– Hallam, G. Butler, George, Martin, Bisarre – Mrs. Butler, Oriana –
Miss Craven, Lemorce – Mrs. Dunning, Ladies – Mrs. Davis, Mrs.
Murray. The afterpiece was *The Jew and The Doctor*. Nothing under full
price was taken.

The programme for the rest of the Race Week was as follows:

Wed. 10th October: *Bold Stroke for a Husband.*
All the World's a Stage.

Nothing under full price.   No admittance behind the scenes.

Ladies and gentlemen that take places, requested to send servants in time to
keep them.

Fri. 12th October: By Desire of the Steward of the Races.
The Road to Ruin.
Tekeli.

Sat. 13th October: *Town and Country.*
Epilogue by Davis and Butler
Young Hussar.

Mon. 15th October: Benefit; Martin, Wilson, Hallam,
Smithson, George, Mrs. Fildew,
Mrs. Murray, Miss Craven.
Soldier's Daughter.
Blind Boy. Blind Boy – Miss Craven.

Wed. 17th October: Benefit; Jefferson, Davis, Dunning,
Bennett, G. Butler, Miss Jefferson.
Busy Body, not here for 10 years.
The Prize.

Fri. 19th October: Last night. Benefit Mr. and Mrs. Butler.
Free Knights. First performance in
Richmond.
Scenery as in Ripon
Christopher – Butler.
Agnes – Mrs. Butler.
A Beggar on Horseback.
Corny Buttercup – Butler.

As for the six performances in Northallerton they included the following plays which were new there: *Grieving's a Folly, Killing No Murder, Foundling of the Forest, Free Knights*. The next port of call after Richmond was Ulverston. The playbills give the customary prices of boxes 3/-, pit 2/-, gallery 1/-. Performances started at seven. The season commenced on 27th October and continued until 29th December, the acting days being Tuesday, Thursday and Saturday except during Xmas week when they were Monday, Wednesday, Thursday and Saturday. There were only two bespeaks: by Lady Mostyn and Miss Jane Machell, Lady Patroness of the Hunt. On 6th December George spoke an occasional address to the ladies and gentlemen of Ulverston. The following plays were advertised as new to the town: Hood's *Killing No Murder* and *Tekeli*, Thomas Dibdin's *Forest of Hermanstadt*, Arnold's *Man and Wife*, Leigh's *Grieving's a Folly*, Hoare's *Three and the Deuce*, Reynolds's *Exile* and *Free Knights*, Kemble's *Plot and Counterplot* and O'Keeffe's *Beggar on Horseback*. *The Grecian Daughter* was revived after 20 years and *The Road to Ruin* after 14. This should mean that Butler had had the town in his circuit as far back as 1790 but these statements on bills are not always strictly accurate. Shakespeare was represented by *Richard III* with the same cast as in Harrogate except for Richard – Bennett, Duke of York – Miss Stoker, Earl of Richmond – by a gentleman for this night only. The cast of the Tate version of *King Lear* differed from that of 1806 in the following particulars: Gloster – Hallam, Kent – G. Butler, Bastard – Wilson, Cornwall – Smithson, Albany – Martin (corrected to Bennett by a Ms. hand). *The Rivals* was also given.

The Hawksworth version of *Oroonoko* (1759) is advertised as depicting 'in the most affecting colours, the Inhumanity of the Slave Trade.' Most astounding of these moral rigmaroles, however, is that for *George Barnwell*. (This advertisement for *George Barnwell* was not confined to Butler's company. Robert Dyer thinks the story was probably a fiction.)[88]

Be warned ye Youths, who see by sad despair,
avoid lewd Women, false as they are fair.

Lillo.

This affecting Tragedy, the moral tendency of which has been so beneficial to the rising generation, is one of the plays lately revived in London. The Manager thinks he cannot better discharge his duty to the inhabitants of Ulverston than by reviving it in this town. Shakespeare says:

Those guilty creatures sitting at a Play,
Have by the very cunning of the Scene,
Been struck to the soul, that presently
They have proclaimed their Malefactions.

Hamlet.

A Story is recorded and the Fact can be proved by many living Witnesses, that a young Gentleman of the City of London, having embezzled part of his Master's property, was providentially at a Representation of George Barnwell at Drury-Lane, when that admirable Actor Mr. Ross personated the character of George Barnwell, at whose fate he was so struck to the soul that it occasioned his immediate contrition and reformation. The Gentleman so benefitted by this excellent Tragedy, was not ashamed of acknowledging his obligation to the Play and Performers, for at every subsequent yearly benefit for Mr. Ross he always received One Hundred Pounds Sterling with a card to the following effect:-
Dear Sir,

One who is indebted to your admirable representation of George Barnwell for more than life, for his redeemed honour and credit, begs your acceptance of the inclosed, which you will receive yearly, so long as you continue in the line of your profession. Happy am I to acknowledge that the Stage has preserved me from ruin [and] disgrace. George Barnwell stopt me in my mad career, and saved me from an ignominious death.

I am your grateful friend and servant,
A Convert.

Where instructions can be blended with amusement, every good parent will be anxious, every master will be desirous, every teacher will recommend the attendance of their pupils. That the Tragedy of George Barnwell exposes vice and its never failing consequences, while it exhorts and stimulates the youth of both sexes to the practice of virtue, the greatest enemy to the theatre will not deny, surely, then, it cannot give offence, if it be earnestly recommended to the heads of families, and indeed earnestly solicited of them, that they will permit the young people under their protection to be present at the representation of the moral, instructive and awful Tragedy of George Barnwell.

Learn to be wise from others' harm,
And you shall do full well.
Lillo.

This play, it may be depended upon, was founded upon fact; the unfortunate hero of the Tragedy, George Barnwell, was executed for the murder of his virtuous and venerable Uncle, to which he was instigated by an artful, cruel and abandoned woman, in the reign of Queen Elizabeth; step by step she led the unwary youth to the cruel deed which terminated a miserable existence by the most ignominious death.

One wonders who stopped to read all this small print on the playbills but one must remember that it was an age of less hurry and less print than our own. Anyhow the theatre's need to justify itself in the eyes of the righteous went to great lengths. Little further information is given about staging though *Tekeli* is said to be 'entirely prepared from Models from the Theatre-Royal Drury Lane' and Holcroft's *Tale of Mystery* with music by Dr. Busby, 'performed in London upwards of 200 nights with unanimous applause,' included a grand fete and a rural dance among its attractions. A rather unusual conclusion to the entertainments on 13th December was:

> . . . a magnificent Display of Fire Works Prepared for the Occasion, and positively for This Night Only: A Brilliant Sun, with various changes, displaying rose, dark angelic Fire. Five Fountains of Chinese Rockets displaying Clusters of blue and Silver Flowers whilst ascending. An Horizontal and Perpendicular Machine, which, after various Changes, represents an Eastern Orange Grove. The Grand Star of Malta, with a vertical Wheel in the Centre. Mr. Dunning respectfully acquaints the Ladies and Gentlemen that these Fireworks are made on so peculiar and safe a Construction without giving the least Offence.

Quite how this elaborate display was given in the narrow confines of a theatre remains a mystery. (Perhaps it never came off at all like a similar display described by Dyer.)[89]

From Ulverston the company went on to Kendal. The playbills announce that children in arms could not be admitted and that good fires had been kept in the theatre. The season opened on 4th January 1811 and the last night but one was on 3rd April. Playing nights were Monday, Wednesday, Friday. In addition to *Africans, Killing No Murder, Three and the Deuce, Exile, Beggar on Horseback* and *Free Knights*, Murphy's *Know your Own Mind* and Dimond's *The Doubtful Son* were advertised as new plays. Shakespeare had a good innings. *Hamlet* was given on 11th February with the following cast: Hamlet – Bennett, King – Wilson, Polonius – Davis, Horatio – Hallam, Laertes – Jefferson, Osric – George, Rosencrantz – Smithson, Guildenstern – G. Butler, Marcellus – Mrs. Martin, Grave-Diggers – Davis, Dunning, Ghost – Butler, Ophelia – Mrs. Jefferson, Player Queen – Mrs. Wilson, Queen – Mrs. Murray. *Macbeth* followed on 13th February:

> . . . as altered and performed at Drury Lane with all the original Music composed by Purcel [*sic*], and Decorations, as now performing in London and Edinburgh, with the greatest Applause.

A laudatory paragraph states:

> Shakespeare was not more remarkable for the dignity of his characters, the strength of his expressions, the elevation of his sentiments, and the natural beauty of his imagery, than for the happy choice of his subjects. In this excellent Tragedy he is more regular than in many of his pieces. It records an important point in the history of Scotland, etc.

The cast was Macbeth – Bennett, Banquo – George, Duncan – Hallam, Malcolm – Jefferson, Seton – Dunning, Lennox – Smithson, Doctor – G. Butler, Officers – Martin, Stoker, Fleance – Master Meadows, Macduff – Wilson, Lady Macbeth – Mrs. Butler, Gentlewomen – Miss Craven, Mrs. Davis, Singing Witches – Mrs. Jefferson, Mrs. Murray, Mrs. Dunning, Hecate – Davis, Speaking Witches – Mrs. Fildew, Mrs. Martin, Miss Jefferson; Apparition of an Armed Head: Master Jefferson, Ditto of a Crowned Head – Master Meadows.

The Merchant of Venice, or The Cruel Jew, was presented on 18th February with the following cast: Shylock – Butler, Bassanio – Bennett, Gratiano – Jefferson, Launcelot – G. Butler, Lorenzo – Smithson, Old Gobbo – George, Salanio – Hallam, Salarino – Dunning, Tubal – Davis, Antonio – Wilson, Jessica with song – Mrs. Jefferson, Nerissa – Miss Craven, Portia – Mrs. Butler.

Richard III had the same cast as in Ulverston except Richmond – Jefferson, Duchess of York – Mrs. Wilson, whilst in *King Lear* Bennett played Albany. *Romeo and Juliet* on 19th March was thus extolled:

> This admired production of the immortal Shakespeare, is one of the most affecting Tragedies ever written – and furnishes such scenes of melting softness, and agonizing love, as the representation alone can convey any idea of, the powers of language being unequal to the task of describing them.

The cast was Romeo – Bennett, Paris – G. Butler, Benvolio – Davis, Friar Lawrence – Wilson, Tybalt – Smithson, Capulet – Hallam, Balthasar – Dunning, Prince – Butler, Montague – Martin, Peter – George, Page – Master Meadows, Mercutio – Jefferson, Lady Capulet – Mrs. Martin, Nurse – Mrs. Fildew, Juliet – Mrs. Butler.

> In Act 1st, A Grand Masquerade. In Act the Fifth, the Funeral Procession of Juliet to the Monument of the Capulets. Accompanied with a Solemn Dirge. Vocal parts by Mr. Davis, Mrs. Jefferson, Mrs. Murray, Mrs. Davis, Mrs. Dunning, &c.

Shakespeare was not the only author to be eulogised. When Colman the Younger's *Battle of Hexham* 'With the Original Songs, Glees, and Chorusses' was given the playbill broke into the following eulogy:

> This most excellent piece is universally and most justly esteemed the first production of the day – The language of the play is most beautifully picturesque and sublime. The comic part of Gregory is highly humourous; which together with the quaint replies of the Fool, produces a most excellent feast for the lovers of mirth, and gives relief to the serious scenes. The moral is good, and upon the whole cannot fail to excite the most agreeable sensation in every feeling mind.

To give one last example which may well compete with the excesses of our film advertising, *Isabella* is said to be 'accounted the best tragedy ever penned since the days of Shakespeare.' The character of Isabella, heightened by her distress for her departed husband and gratitude for Villeroy, her admirer, is one of the most affecting pieces of dramatic writing. Words must fall short of the tender scene, where her supposed deceased husband returns, and finds her married to Villeroy. The cruelty of her father-in-law; the falsehood of Carlos; and the fatal deaths of Biron and Isabella, the heart may feel; but 'tis impossible for the tongue to describe.'

For Garrick's pantomime *Harlequin's Invasion* the following transformations and effects were advertised:

In Act the first The Trick of the Fork. The Magical Tree which changes to Snip, the Taylor.

In Act Second The three Justices changed to Three Old Women. A Song, by the Principal Old Woman. Harlequin, as a Friar, changes to a Brazen Head. The Statue of Shakespeare, Which rises in the Temple of Fame as Harlequin, Sinks on Mercury waving his Caduceus. To conclude with the favourite song of the Mulberry Tree.

And several of the principal characters in Shakespeare's Plays will appear on the Stage, Sir John Falstaff, King Richard, Hamlet, Shylock, Touchstone, Audrey, Mrs. Ford, Mrs. Page, Ophelia, Benedict, Beatrice, etc.

Mr. Kerr's playbills have taken us through the company's activities for a year and a month. During this time they presented 36 comedies, 14 farces, 12 tragedies, 11 musical farces, 9 plays, 8 melodramas, 4 operatic pieces, 2 pantomimes, 2 comic operas, 1 dramatic romance and 1 musical entertainment. The most popular play was the melodrama *Tekeli* with 16 performances; after that came *Killing No Murder* with 11, *Blue Beard* with 9, *Three and the Deuce, Free Knights, Beggar on Horseback* and *Bold Stroke for a Husband* with 7, and *Grieving's A Folly, Honeymoon, Animal Magnetism, Inconstant, All the World's a Stage, Jew and the Doctor, Africans, Foundling of the Forest, Blind Boy, Exile* and *Young Hussar* with 6. Most of these were new plays and were therefore given at each town in turn. Shakespeare did not fare so well, there being only 3 performances of *Richard III*, 2 of *Lear* and 1 each of *Hamlet, Macbeth, Romeo and Juliet, Merchant of Venice*. Yet though George Colman was the most popular author with 10 pieces, Shakespeare, Morton and Mrs. Inchbald took second place with 6; O'Keeffe and Dimond followed with 5 and Prince Hoare with 4. The number of benefits given in the various circuit towns were: 12 in Ripon, 7 in Beverley, 9 in Harrogate, 3 in Richmond, 18 in Ulverston, 15 in Kendal. There does not appear to have been any system in these. Butler took five and Mrs. Butler five and they had one together. Husbands and wives usually shared a benefit but occasionally had separate ones. Take for example, the Dunnings; they each had one to themselves, they had four together and two shared with others, whilst Dunning had one shared with others in which Mrs. Dunning did not participate. Of the others who had solo benefits Mrs. Fildew, Miss Jefferson and Miss Craven had two each whilst Bennett, Jefferson, Mrs. Jefferson and G. Butler had one each. Occasionally benefits were failures and the actors were allowed a second chance. Thus Bennett and Wilson advertised in Ripon that 'having fail'd in the former attempts, Mr. Butler has favour'd them with another Night, hoping it will meet the approbation of the public.' The Bennetts came from Edinburgh. Bennett remained with the company, playing leading roles until 1812 but Mrs. Sarah Bennet died in October, 1810. The company during this period consisted of 11 men, 12 women and 2 children besides W. and T. Mercer, Kelly and the Stagekeeper who did not act but had benefits. As we have seen supers were occasionally enlisted for spectacular pieces.

Probably the company's spring season was spent at Northallerton, which seems to have alternated with Ripon.

By June 1811 they were again in Harrogate and I have playbills for their season there between 25th June and 15th August, though probably the season began before this as it certainly ended after. At least three guest artists were engaged. On 29th June Butler, after paying his:

> ... respects to the Ladies and Gentlemen at Harrogate and KnaresBro' Begs leave to inform them he has engaged Mr. Phillip's [sic] from the Theatre-Royal, York, to perform Six Nights, prior to his engagement in London, and flatters himself that it will meet with their approbation and Support.

Among his parts were Duke of Aranza in *The Honeymoon*, Reuben Glenroy in *Town and Country*, Capt. Irwin in *Everyone has his Fault*, Romaldi in *A Tale of Mystery*, Joseph Surface in *The School for Scandal* and Rosenberg in *Ella Rosenberg*. Mrs. Jordan was engaged for two nights, when prices were raised to boxes 4/-, pit 2/6d, the gallery remaining at 1/-. On 15th August she played Lady Teazle to the Sir Peter of Butler. I have not the playbill for the second night. On Tuesday, 27th August the Rev. James Tate wrote to his wife from the Crown:

> I saw Miss *Duncan* then on Thursday night in the *Jealous Wife* & in the *Romp* – greatly amusing in both. – – – By the way, *Mr. Butler* dines with me tomorrow; and I with him on Friday. Poor Miss *Jefferson* has half a benefit tonight: and by a note to the *Doctor* – such is the title my hat gives me – implores my interest with the Ladies & Gentlemen of the Crown a task of all others to me most ungracious. – But the *Doctor* must not recruit for the Play-house.

Maria Duncan, later Mrs. Davison, was a gifted comedy actress, and the original Juliana in Tobin's *Honeymoon*, a pleasing singer and graceful dancer, she was a favourite in the York circuit.

Plays new to Harrogate were Masters's *Lost and Found*, Holman's *Gazette Extraordinary*, Millingen's *Beehive* (all London 1811), Dimond's *Doubtful Son* (London 1810), Greffulhe's *Is He A Prince?* (London 1809). The *Suspicious Husband* was revived after 20 years and *Isabella* after 26 years. This latter would take us back to the season in which Jane Wallis acted as a child. New players were Metcalfe, who left the same year, and Miss Wood who may have been a sister of Mrs. George Jefferson's. She married T. Mercer in 1814 and was still in the company in 1815 but her name disappears after that.

Two playbills for the 1811 season at Richmond are in the Harvard Theatre Collection. On 8th October Holman's comedy *The Gazette Extraordinary* made its debut there with Mrs. Butler as Lady Juliet Sandford and Butler as Dr. Suitall followed by *Rosina* with the Jeffersons as Rosina and William. On 14th October *The Jew* was given at the desire of the gentlemen of the Grammar School with Butler as Sheva and was followed by a recitation by Butler of Shakespeare's *Seven Ages of Man* and then by *High Life below Stairs*. Timothy Hutton records in his Diary attendances at the plays at Richmond on 26th September and 1st November.

The 21 nights of subscription at Whitby opened on 20th November 1811 and the season closed rather later than usual on 28th February 1812. Days of playing were Monday, Wednesday and Friday. Thwaites is still mentioned as scene painter and was presumably a local man who provided for the company whilst they were in Whitby. During the season the company played 21 comedies, 12 melodramas, 11 farces, 9 tragedies, 8 plays, 8 musical farces, 5 comic operas, 4 pantomimes, 1 ballad opera, 1 burletta, 1 dramatic opera and 1 interlude. The growth in popularity of melodrama is to be noted. The most frequently played authors were Dimond and Colman the Younger with 7 pieces each, Shakespeare and Morton with 5 and Mrs. Inchbald with 4. Shakespeare plays were *Richard III*, *Othello*, *Merchant of Venice*, *Hamlet* and *Macbeth*. Plays new to Whitby which had been given in London in 1811, were Millingen's *Beehive*, Dimond's *Royal Oak*, Miss Chambers's *Ourselves*, Masters's *Lost and Found*, Holman's *Gazette Extraordinary*, Morton's *Knight of Snowdoun;* and those given in London in 1810 were Dimond's *Doubtful Son*, Greffulhe's *Budget of Blunders*, Reynolds's *Free Knights*, Pocock's *Hit and Miss* and Rhodes's *Bombastes Furioso*. Two pantomimes, Fawcett's *Perouse* and *Oscar and Malvina* seem to have been new to this company since nothing under full price was taken when they were performed. The following made their first appearance: Collier, Shelmerdine and Mortimer, whilst Master Stoker

61

was added to the list of children. The company opened in Ripon on 5th March with *Hit and Miss*, *Ways and Means* and *Killing No Murder*. Charles Mathews, the comedian, was engaged for three nights during which nothing under full price was taken.

From here the company moved to Beverley and there on 15th June 1812 Samuel Butler died.[90] The obituary notice in the *York Chronicle* speaks of him as:

> . . . for many years manager of the Theatres at Beverley, Harrogate, Ripon, Kendal and Whitby: a gentleman much respected by a numerous circle of friends, and whose death is a severe and irreparable loss to his family.

Butler was buried at St. Mary's Church and a memorial tablet to him in the south transept reads:

> In memory of Samuel Butler 'a poor player, that struts and frets his hour upon the stage, and then is heard no more!' Obt. 15 June, 1812. aet. 62.

Butler's death must have been a grievous blow yet the company seems to have carried right on since Mr. Sheppard lists a bill for 22nd June when *The Heir at Law* and *Oscar and Malvina* were played.[91] Butler's son, Samuel William, was only nine years old but his second wife, as her predecessor had done in similar circumstances, shouldered the responsibility and ran the company herself for the next six years.

CHAPTER IV

The Decline and Fall of the Butlers, 1812 – 30

ACCORDING TO WALTER DONALDSON (p. 176) the circuit became disjointed and the company disorganised after Butler's death. He says that Miss Lawrence of Ripon, who was a member of the de Gray family, took what remained of the establishment under her protection and settled on each performer 25 guineas a year, that is on Mrs. Butler, her daughter Mrs. Percy, Martin the prompter and his wife, Jefferson and old George who had been with the company 50 years. But this must refer to something that happened many years later. Miss Butler did not become Mrs. Percy or Piercy until 1821; but though George was still with the company in 1823, we do not hear of the Martins after 1817. I incline to believe, that if this story is true at all, it must have taken place about 1819 at a time when the company, as we shall see, was in great difficulties. At first everything appears to have gone smoothly under Mrs. Butler's direction. The company moved on to Harrogate, playing there by 14th July. The men were Collier, Bennett, Wilson, Smithson, Jefferson, G. Butler, Hallam, George, Martin, Mortimer, Stoker, Meadows. This last played juvenile parts and was probably Drinkwater Meadows who had first appeared with the company as a child in 1801. The women were Mrs. Butler, Miss Craven, Mrs. and Miss Jefferson, Miss Wood, Mrs. Murray, Mrs. Fildew, Miss Stoker. Mrs. Butler continued to act and the few playbills we have of this season give her as Mrs. Ferment in *The School of Reform*, Lady Mathilda Wyndham in *Royal Oak* and Mrs. Mortimer in *Laugh When you Can*. Several of the new plays were produced. Morton's *Knight of Snowdoun* was performed 'with the Original Scotch Music, Dresses, and appropriate Scenery.' The scenery consisted of 'The Lake. Rocky Promontories, &c. &c. The Sylvan Bower. The Goblin's Cave, and The Fort.' On 23rd July, Dimond's *Royal Oak* and Greffulhe's *Budget of Blunders* were acted for the first time here and on 25th July Fawcett's pantomime *Perouse* appeared and was treated to the following playbill puff:

> The universal satisfaction and applause this esteemed and admired
> Piece everywhere creates, leaves little room for a commentator to dwell

on. The incidents with which it is replete, so rapidly follow each other, that the mind constantly employed in admiration, has no time to balance the preference due to either of them.

The Dunnings had left the company and we do not know who succeeded Dunning as scene painter. Presumably Mrs. Butler continued the circuit to Richmond and Ulverston.

At Kendal *Hamlet* was given on 27th February with Bennett as Hamlet, Wilson as the King, Mortimer as Polonius, Hallam as Horatio, Collier as Laertes, G. Butler and Mortimer as the Gravediggers, Jefferson as the Ghost, Miss Wood as Ophelia and Mrs. Murray as the Queen. On 22nd March it was the turn of *Othello* with Bennett in the title role, Wilson as Iago, Jefferson as Cassio, Mrs. Butler as Desdemona and Mrs. Murray as Emilia. On 1st March, Kendal first witnessed the pantomime of *Oscar and Malvina*.

There are no records this year from Northallerton or Beverley but by 10th August 1813 the company were again in the midst of their season at Harrogate. Performances were given by desire of the Ladies and Gentlemen of the White Hart and of the Crescent. On 14th August the part of Alonzo in *Pizarro* was taken by a gentleman from Knaresborough being his first attempt on any stage. *Pizarro* was followed by the new farce *How to Die for Love* adapted from Kotzebue and produced in London in 1812. Oulton's farce *The Sleep Walker*, also given in London 1812, was another new piece. The company had lost one of their leading men, Bennett, but Bywater, who had not been with them since 1806, re-appeared. Miss Butler, who had not played since 1807 and was now about 13 years old returned as a dancer in the interludes between the play and the afterpiece.

A Richmond playbill on satin for 8th November 1813, gives *The Clandestine Marriage*, not acted there for many years, and *Raising the Wind*.[92] The comedy had the following cast: Ogleby – George, Lovewell – Collier, Sir John Melville – Smithson, Brush – Jefferson, Canton – Meadows, Sterling – Hallam, Mrs. Heidleberg – Mrs. Murray, Miss Sterling – Miss Craven, Betty – Miss Wood, Chambermaid – Miss Hord, Fanny – Mrs. Butler, The farce's cast was: Plainway – Hallam, Diddler – Jefferson, Fainwould – Meadows, Sam – Bywater, John – Martin, Waiter – Davis, Richard – George, Peggy – Mrs. Jefferson, Miss Durable – Mrs. Fildew. Miss Butler recited Collins's *Ode to the Passions* between the two and Jefferson and Miss Hord sang. Miss Hord and Davis were new members of the company. Tickets were to be had of Mrs. Butler at Mrs. Marshall's near the theatre.

When Mrs. Butler opened her season at Whitby on 23rd November 1813, she informed the public that no effort would be spared on her part to render the theatre worthy of their attention. There was a 21 nights' subscription and the season continued until 18th March, a month longer than usual. Mr. Wilson from the Royal Amphitheatre was engaged for three nights to perform on the tight rope. Among his feats was that of walking on a rope from the stage to the back of the gallery and back again wheeling a real barrow.

The season was remarkable for the large number of tragedies given: there were 25 comedies, 13 farces, 11 tragedies, 9 melodramas, 6 plays, 6 pantomimes, 5 musical farces, 4 comic operas, 2 ballad operas, 1 opera and 1 burletta. Colman the Younger still headed the list with 6 plays, Dimond and O'Keeffe each had 5, Mrs. Inchbald and Kenney 4 and Shakespeare only 2 (*Richard III* and *Romeo and Juliet* with Mrs. Butler as Juliet). Coleridge's *Remorse* was given on 23rd December. An otherwise unknown serious pantomime *Black Forest or The Robbers of the Cave* was presented on 28th February. Plays new to London in 1813 were Morton's *Education*, Coleridge's *Remorse*, Jameson's *Students of Salamanca*, Thomas Dibdin's *Orange Boven*, and Pocock's famous *Miller and his Men*; new to London in 1812 were *How to Die for Love*, Kenney's *Turn Out*, Mrs. Lefanu's *Sons of Erin* and Oulton's *Sleep Walker*. The Butler children both took part in the performances. Miss Butler played Little Red Riding Hood and Little Pickle in *The Spoil'd Child* and Master Butler sang a song being his first attempt in this kind. Later than usual in July the company was in Beverley and gave *Richard III* and *The Prize* on the 6th of that month.[93] I have a number of playbills for this 1814 season in Harrogate. The players were here too rather later than in other years and the bills cover a period from 20th August to 4th October which was the last night but two. Sieur Sanches, the rope dancer was engaged in September. He was advertised to 'Walk with his Feet against the Ceiling over the Stage, and his Head Downwards,' to perform various feats on the slack rope and to perform 'On the Spanish Guitar, and Accompany himself, with the Imitation of the melodious notes of various Birds, etc.' For this treat the price of the boxes and upper boxes rose to 4/-. This price was also charged at Mrs. Butler's benefit when those two favourite melodramas *The Miller and His Men* and *Timour the Tartar* were given first performances in Harrogate. Once again a gentleman from Knaresborough performed, this time as Douglas. Hook's *Darkness Visible* and a new and otherwise unknown pantomime called *Harlequin Sundial* were presented for the first time on 3rd September. A 'Prospectus of the principal Scenes, Tricks and Incidents' of the pantomime is given:

Scene I. Enchanted Garden – A general Transformation, occasioned by the Magic Touch of a Fairy's Wand; and by which a Sun-Dial becomes Harlequin. Spring is changed to Columbine. – Frost is metamorphosed into Pantaloon; and the Figure of Time is changed to that of Clown. Scene II. Sea Coast – A Voyage, and Narrow Escape – A new Mode of Fishing. Scene III. – Street. – Scene IV. – Inside of a Tavern –

Vanishing Table Cloths. Scene V. Street – Pursuit. Scene VI. Street – A Gold Beater's Shop – The animated Golden Arm. Pantaloon's Death, and astonishing Restoration to Life, after two Buckets of Water poured down his Throat. Scene VII. – A Dark Forest – A Robber is vanquished, and compelled to restore his Booty. – Scene VIII. – A Barber's Shop – The wonderful Effects of Russia Oil on a Hair Broom – the Lover's Disaster – Scene IX. – The Humours of a Country Fair in which is introduced a Variety of Comical Characters – Pantaloon and Lover tortured by Wild Beasts. Scene X. – Dungeon – Harlequin deceived by Will-O'-the-Wisp – looses [sic] his Power, but is afterwards restored by the Interference of the good Genii. – Scene XI. – Genii's Palace. – A Reconciliation. The whole to conclude with Chorus, &c.

Master Butler played Harlequin, Miss Butler Columbine, Wilson Pantaloon and Jefferson Clown. *Little Red Riding Hood* was given on 6th September with Miss Butler as the heroine, Master Butler as the Shepherd Boy, George as Grandmamma and Hallam as Wolf. Dibdin's *Orange Boven* 'with appropriate Scenery and Decorations' was presented on 17th September with Mrs. Butler as Britannia, Miss Butler as Peace and Master Butler as a Sailor. Master Butler also played a Servant in *Darkness Visible*, Barber in the *Weathercock*, Waiter in *Laugh When You Can*, John in *The Agreeable Surprise*, Cook in *Turn Out*, Zingra in *Miller and His Men*, Abdalec in *Timour the Tartar* and Kangaroo in *Perouse*. Other children who performed were Master Jefferson, Master F. Jefferson and Master Stoker. Thomas Mercer who had married Miss Wood also appeared on the stage though previously he had been with the company only in a supernumerary capacity of some sort. Errington was a new actor. Timothy Hutton attended a play at Richmond on Saturday, 15th October 1814 as recorded in his *Diary*.

On 12th April 1815 F. C. Wemyss joined the Company at Kendal and he has left us a description which enables us to catch a fleeting view of it from within.[94] Wemyss was introduced to Mrs. Butler by her brother George Jefferson who was at that time stage manager. Possibly he had taken over these onerous duties after the death of Butler. Wemyss tells us that Morton's *School of Reform* and Colman's *We Fly by Night* were billed for the benefit of Meadows for the following evening; he then continues:

I waited upon Mrs. Butler, stating my views and wishes, when she informed me Mr. Thomas Mercer was on the point of leaving the company; but, being a total stranger to my talent, she must require a specimen of my abilities, before she could make me an offer of any description. It was therefore agreed that I should play Henry in *Speed the Plough*, for Mr. Hallam's benefit, on Wednesday evening. At the theatre I was introduced; it was a neat building, regularly built, and capable of holding from sixty to seventy pounds. I was much pleased with the manner in which the business was conducted. Meadows played Tyke, with a feeling and talent rarely seen in a country theatre, and the whole performance was such as to make me anxious to become a member of the company. On Wednesday, I appeared in Henry to a house fortunately well filled. The actor being a favourite the *debut* was pronounced so promising that I was offered fifteen shillings per week, the highest salary given, which I cheerfully accepted, really happy to think I had obtained a situation. The following ladies and gentlemen composed the company:- Mr. G. Jefferson, stage manager; Mr. Brewer, Mr. Meadows, Mr. Mercer, Mr. Hallam, Mr. George, Mr. Martin, Mr. Bristow, Mr. J. O'Connor, Master Samuel Butler, Mr. Stoker, Mrs. Butler, Mrs. Murray, Mrs. Mercer, Miss Craven, Miss Stoker, Miss Butler, Mrs. Martin.

During Passion Week the licensed theatres were closed but this did not prevent the actors dividing into small parties of four or five and visiting villages in the neighbourhood which seldom had the opportunity of seeing plays performed. Wemyss joined a party consisting of Mercer, Meadows, J. O'Connor, Mrs. Murray and Miss Craven. They went to Kirby Lonsdale and having announced *George Barnwell*, discovered that their number was too small to complete the cast. They solved the difficulty by asking William Mercer who was the leader of the orchestra and who had accompanied them on their enterprise, to make his first appearance on the stage as the Uncle. Though he was but 25 years of age he was always insisting that the young lads knew nothing of acting. But his pride had a fall because he was struck with stage fright and could hardly utter a word; when he spoke, he spoke well but with a broad Yorkshire accent. Poor William's memory only returned after the prompter had rung down the curtain.

From Kendal the company went on to Northallerton and Wemyss gives us an insight into the hardships a travelling company endured:

This distance is something over sixty miles, which, on a fine summer morning, in company with O'Connor, Meadows, William Mercer, and Mr. Kelly I started to walk. We allowed ourselves two days to accomplish the task, walking twenty miles before breakfast the first day, fourteen to dinner, and fourteen after dinner; thus accomplishing forty-eight miles the first day over a mountainous country, and leisurely walking fifteen miles on the following day. So accustomed had I become to fatigue of this description, that a walk of thirty miles was no common occurrence for a day's amusement, when we had no act at night.

Six weeks at Northallerton was followed by Race Week at Beverley and then by the Harrogate summer season. Here Booth was engaged and acted three nights at Harrogate and three at Ripon in the same week. 'His performance of Bertram at this time,' says Wemyss (in Maturin's tragedy which had only just been produced in London), 'was terrifically grand; he left us all delighted with his acting and equally well pleased with himself off the stage.' On 5th June the company lost Mrs. Mary Fildew who died at the age of 69 and was buried in Richmond churchyard.[95]

From Harrogate Wemyss went with the company to Richmond, crossed to Northallerton for Race Week and returned to Richmond. Butler's 10 years lease of the Richmond Theatre was not due to expire until 1819 but Mrs. Butler applied for a renewal in December 1815 and on 6th December the Corporation granted an additional term of 11 years from May Day 1819 under the covenants and conditions of the original lease.[96] Why she applied so far in advance is not evident. The winter season was spent in Whitby where the company acted from 26th December 1815, until 6th April 1816. But before that Mrs. Butler had engaged Mr. Moritz and his company for three nights for conjuring (grandiloquently called philosophical and mathematical experiments), balancing and ventriloquism, the last night being on 24th November. Moritz himself took the theatre for two more nights at the reduced prices of boxes 2/-, pit 1/-, gallery 6d. On 1st January, a bullet and glass bottle were thrown into the orchestra and onto the stage and on 5th January the playbill announced that 'By order of the Magistrates, Constables will attend the Theatre to maintain peace and regularity.' Sieur Sanches was once again engaged to perform his imitations of musical instruments and tricks on the slack rope on 29th January, his last night and benefit being on 5th February. On this night he directed an otherwise unknown serious pantomime entitled *The Indians or the Punishment of Treachery*. On 6th April, the last night of the season, Jefferson presented a few amateurs in a miscellaneous entertainment called *The Thespian Jubilee* and a pantomime, otherwise unknown, called *The Miser, or the Mysterious Purse of Gold* in which Miss Butler joined the amateurs as Columbine. Prices were reduced on this occasion. During the season 19 comedies, 18 farces, 12 melodramas, 9 tragedies, 9 musical farces, 6 pantomimes, 4 plays, 2 comic operas and 1 interlude were performed. Thomas Dibdin and Colman the Younger headed the list with 6 pieces, and Shakespeare followed with 5 (*Richard III, Macbeth, Othello, Merchant of Venice, Hamlet*). Plays new to London in 1815 were Dibdin's *Past Ten O'Clock*, Pocock's *Magpie or the Maid*, Poole's *Who's Who;* new to London in 1814 were: S. J. Arnold's *Woodman's Hut, Jean de Paris*, Dibdin's *Forest of Bondy* and *Ninth Statue*, Kerr's *Wandering Boys* and Leigh's *Where to Find a Friend*. George Jefferson also branched into authorship and his *Variety* was produced on 6th March. The prologue to his effort is printed in his *Theatrical Eccentricities*.[97] Of the new actors Wemyss is advertised as from Glasgow, J. O'Connor from Dublin, Young from Nottingham, Miss Stannard from Lincoln; there were in addition F. O'Connor, Mrs. and Miss O'Connor, and another scion of the Jeffersons, Master. C. Jefferson, who was the third of their boys to appear on the stage. Young was a stage name for Frederick Baltimore Calvert, who was later to become known by his pamphlet *A Defence of the Acted Drama in a Letter Addressed to the Rev. Thomas Best of Sheffield.*[98]

The company's spring campaign was in Ripon. A bill in my possession for 16th April gives *The Mountaineers* with Young as Octavian and Miss Butler as Zorayda, followed by *Harlequin Sundial* with F. O'Connor as Harlequin, Wemyss as Gardener afterwards Lover, J. O'Connor as Winter afterwards Pantaloon, Meadows as Time afterwards Clown, and Miss Butler as Spring afterwards Columbine. After leaving Ripon Wemyss tells us that the company progressed to Beverley, Harrogate, Richmond and thence over the mountains to Ulverston and Kendal. Either the Beverley season must have been very short or Wemyss is in error about a visit this year, because on 27th May 1816, Messrs. Anderson and Faulkner, who described themselves in a playbill as strangers, took over the Beverley Theatre.[99] It is interesting that their scenery was painted by Thwaites and Jefferson, which suggests that it was the stock scenery of Mrs. Butler's company. The company probably had certain stock scenes at every theatre in their circuit.

The loss of Beverley was the beginning of a decline which was to end in the breaking up of the circuit; it is the first symptom that things were not going as well as they should with the company.

Sometime during this period Mrs. Butler engaged Mrs. Renaud, better known as Mrs. Powell of Drury Lane. (She married Renaud in 1814.)[98] Wemyss[99] says that:

> Her acting spoke more to the heart than that of any lady I ever saw before or since, identifying herself with the character she was performing, until you forgot the woman in the actress.

He played Jaffier to her Belvidera and tells a charming anecdote of the help she gave him on that occasion:

> I had requested her indulgence in the morning at the rehearsal, on two accounts – the first, the short time I had allowed for preparation and the second the consciousness of my inability to support her properly, but that I would do the best I could with a part far beyond my ability, and of which I knew nothing but the words. In the kindest manner, she repeated the part to me, impressing upon my mind those portions of the dialogue usually producing the greatest effect upon an audience – to her tuition I owed the success of my performance; and as we left the stage, at the end of the first act, her expression of 'Very well, indeed, sir – excellent', enabled me to proceed with that confidence which, in an actor, is the sure forerunner of success.

The press complimented him and the manager condescended to thank him in the green room afterwards. Mrs. Renaud remained with the company for a year, playing a few nights in each town, among her parts being Elvira in *Pizarro*, Alicia in *Jane Shore* and Lady Macbeth in which Wemyss pronounces her, not so powerful as, but second only to, Mrs. Siddons. Mrs. Renaud left the company at Kendal in 1817 to join the Edinburgh company with whom she remained until her death in 1831.[100]

The season at Kendal opened on 12th March and Mrs. Butler not only announced the engagement of Mrs. Renaud 'whose distinguished talents are so universally acknowledged' for a few nights but promised that during the two months' season 'every successful novelty will be produced.'[101] Fires had been kept in the theatre to secure warmth for the audience. Mrs. Renaud played Lady Macbeth on 15th March and Hamlet, as she had performed it in London, Dublin and Edinburgh, for her benefit on 24th March, as well as Constance in the Mad Scene from *King John* and Yarico in *Inkle and Yarico*. On 5th April Mrs. Butler announced that she had re-engaged Mrs. Renaud who appeared that evening as Volumnia in *Coriolanus* with the following supporting cast: Coriolanus – Young, Cominius – F. O'Connor, Agrippa – Meadows, Sicinius – George, Brutus – O'Connor, Aufidius – Wemyss, Y. Marcius – Miss. L. Stoker, Volusius – Jefferson, Virgilia – Miss Butler, Valeria – Miss Craven. This was the first performance of the tragedy in Kendal and the playbill advertised it in this paragraph:

> Dr. Johnson says the Tragedy of *Coriolanus* is one of the most amusing of our Author's Performances. The Hero and Heroine of this Drama are both so inimitably drawn, that it is impossible not to feel the deepest interest in their conflicts.

On this evening too Mrs. Renaud recited the Monody on the Death of Sir John Moore, in the character of a British Officer.

The afterpiece was *Pitcairn's Island* 'with new Scenery, Dresses and Decorations.' A paragraph in the *Westmorland Advertiser* for 5th April says of this piece that 'the novelty of the subject cannot fail to excite general curiosity'; of the company in general it states that 'by Mrs. Butler's attention to the abilities and characters of her Theatrical assistants, the present company of comedians is truly respectable.' On 14th April *The Earl of Essex* was revived after 20 years with Young as Essex, Wemyss as Southampton, Mrs. Renaud as Queen Elizabeth and Miss Butler as the Countess of Rutland.

For Mrs. Butler's benefit on 19th April *The Magpie or The Maid* was presented in Kendal for the first time.

> The Scenery entirely new and appropriate, designed and painted by Mr. J.O'Connor. Outside a Farm House and a Yard at Palaiseau. – Exterior of a Church. Court of Justice. – A Pastoral Dance – The Magpie steals a piece of Plate.

After this the Statue Scene from *A Winter's Tale* was played with Mrs. Renaud as Hermione, Wemyss as Leontes, F. O'Connor as Florizel, Miss Butler as Perdita and Miss Craven as Paulina.

Then came the *Maid of the Oaks* with Mrs. Butler as Lady Bab, and lastly Farley's melodrama *Aladdin* with the following scenery:

The Magician's Study. – Interior of a Mystic Cavern, in which is discovered the Wonderful Lamp. Cottage of Aladdin's Mother. Apartment of the Princess – Exterior of the Royal Bath. Chinese Bridge, over which passes the grand Procession prepared for Aladdin by the Genius of the Lamp. Aladdin's superb Magical Flying Palace.

A very full evening's entertainment. The *Westmorland Advertiser* spoke of Mrs. Butler as:

. . . long the deservedly respected in this town, for her theatrical abilities and attention to every social duty. The novelty of the performance which has never been acted here with the addition of new and splendid scenery, will, it is hoped, insure a full audience.

On 28th April Mrs. Renaud appeared as Euphrasia in *The Grecian Daughter*, on 29th April as the Queen in *Richard III* and on 19th May as Cephania in Dimond's *Aethiop*, which was played for the first time in Kendal. The scenery was as follows:

Turkish Burying Ground. – Chamber of Haroun Alraschid – Alexis is seen driving his camel towards the Bazestein – Cephania's galley approaches the shore.

This was for Jefferson's benefit and he had devised thereafter an entertainment called *Bits and Scraps* a vocal medley, which he compiled, arranged and sang. On 26th May Mrs. Renaud played Catherine in *Catherine and Petruchio*.

Miss Butler had her benefit on 3rd June and the *Westmorland Advertiser* inserted a paragraph that:

. . . the acknowledged talents of this Juvenile Actress, will undoubtedly insure to her that portion of the public favours, which she certainly merits.

Leigh's *Where to find a Friend* was given its first performance in Kendal that night and was followed by the *Statue Scene*, a song by Master F. Jefferson, his second appearance, *The Sultan* and *The Wandering Boys* another particularly long programme.

Mrs. Renaud had a second benefit on 9th June when she played the famous role of Lady Imogine in Maturin's *Bertram* to the Bertram of Young and the St. Aldebrande of Wemyss. She followed this by playing Dame Scout in *The Village Lawyer* and Hermione in the statue scene. That she was popular in Kendal is testified by the *Westmorland Advertiser* which states that her 'theatrical abilities are at present properly appreciated and generally admired in the vicinity of Kendal.' Her benefit was to have been her last night but on 23rd June she appeared as Julia in *The Rivals* for the benefit of Mrs. Jefferson and on 30th June at the desire of Mrs. Harrison she appeared again as Hamlet with the following supporting cast: King –O'Connor, Polonius – George, Horatio – F. O'Connor, Laertes – Wemyss, Rosencrantz – Martin, 1st Gravedigger – Master Butler, 2nd Gravedigger – Stoker, Ghost – Young, Ophelia – Miss Stannard, Queen – Mrs. Murray, Player Queen – Mrs. Martin.

The season finally came to an end on 7th July with a reproduction of the Grand Masquerade as given at the London theatres:

The entire Stage will be formed so as to represent a most Picturesque Temple. Terminating with a Bower Brilliantly Illuminated. Transparencies, Devices – A Drop Scene, the Masks arriving &c Ludicrous Incidents on their Entrance. The Masquerade Scene, Fete Champetre at Night, Beautifully illuminated with coloured Lamps and Transparencies, discovering numerous Masks in groups, and various Devices will diversify the Scene.

So successful had the season been that Mrs. Butler, instead of playing two months as originally planned had stayed nearly four, yet the company was never to return to Kendal.

Meanwhile on 20th January 1817, the Richmond Theatre was the scene of an amateur performance for the relief of the poor by desire of the ladies of Richmond. A playbill for this occasion gives Colman's play *John Bull*, the farce *To Die for Love* and a musical farce whose name is unfortunately missing. All parts were taken by young men.[102]

An echo from times past was the death of Fielding Wallis at Kirby Stephen on 15th March 1817 at the age of 63. He was buried in Richmond Churchyard.

Wemyss was still in the company when they visited Harrogate as usual in the summer. Two playbills in my possession for this year give, on 22nd July, Morton's *Way to Get Married* with Master Butler as Dashall and Miss Butler as Julia Faulkner followed by the first performance there of Oulton's *My Landlady's Gown* 'Performed with unprecedented attraction last Season, in London.' In this Wemyss played Jack Jocund, Young Mons. Genlis, Master Butler Timothy Bulton and Miss Butler Laurette. On 24th July *The Rivals* was given with the following cast: Sir Anthony Absolute – George, Faulkland – Young, Capt. Absolute – Wemyss, Acres – Jefferson, Sir Lucius O'Trigger – O'Connor, Fag – F. O'Connor, David – Master Butler, Coachman – Martin, William – Stoker, Mrs. Malaprop – Mrs. Murray, Lydia Languish – Miss Butler, Lucy – Miss Craven, Julia – Mrs. Butler. This was followed by the farce *Trick for Trick* in which Wemyss played Young Heartwell and Miss Butler Eliza. Days of playing were Tuesday, Thursday, and Saturday.

Soon after this Wemyss left the company. He had formed an attachment to Miss Butler who was then about 17. Wemyss himself being scarcely 20 their extreme youth was the objection to their marriage and it was agreed that they should separate for twelve months, and, if they remained steadfast, should be united. Despite eternal vows they never saw each other again.

Whilst Wemyss was in the company it underwent considerable changes in personnel, losing Meadows, Hallam, Mr. and Mrs. Mercer, Brewer, Bristow and Miss Craven and replacing them by Young, and O'Connors and Miss Stannard.

Mrs. Butler did not open in Whitby until 21st January 1818 and she remained there until 10th April. (Wilson, late of the Birmingham Theatre, ran a month's season there from 12th Sept. – 9th Oct. 1817.) That her season there was not altogether unsuccessful is proved by the fact that she was due to close on 18th March but on that night the playbill announced:

> Mrs. Butler begs leave to inform the ladies and gentlemen of Whitby and the Public in general that its being the wish of several of her friends (in consequence of the shortness of the season) the Theatre will continue open a few more nights.

George Young writing in 1817 said:

> Sometimes the house, which will seat about 500 is well filled: at other times the performers complain of want of encouragement; but whether this is owing to an increasing taste for other pleasures, or to other causes, I will not determine.[103]

There were failures too in benefits, and though this had happened before, when taken along with Young's statement, it seems to indicate that the company was not so flourishing as it had been.

For the first time Samuel Butler's name appears in the benefit list; at the age of 15 he was regarded as an adult player and acted such parts as Malcolm in *Macbeth*, Laertes in *Hamlet* and Roderigo in *Othello*.

The season being shorter than usual, the range of plays was necessarily less. Fifteen comedies, 11 melodramas, 9 farces, 9 tragedies, 5 musical farces, 3 plays, 2 comic operas, 2 pantomimes, 1 ballet and 1 burletta were performed. Morton and Dibdin were the favourite authors with 5 plays apiece and Shakespeare and Dimond followed with 4. The Shakespeare plays were *Richard III*, *Macbeth*, *Hamlet* and *Othello* with Young in the title roles of the last two. There was no slackening in the production of new plays: those brought out in London in 1817 were Oulton's *Frightened to Death* and Sheil's *Apostate*; those which appeared in London in 1816 were

Maturin's *Bertram*, Morton's *Slave*, Dimond's *Broken Sword*, Dibdin's *What Next* and *Pitcairn's Island*, Terry's *Guy Mannering*, and Oulton's *My Landlady's Gown*.

Considerable changes had again taken place in the company's personnel. Howell from Liverpool, Chiswell from Glasgow, the Golds from Edinburgh and Driver had joined it. The Martins, who had been with the company for so long, had left and so had Wemyss and Miss Stannard. By the Harrogate season in September there is again a fresh crop of names. Pope, Osbaldiston, Holmes, Webber and Mr. and Mrs. Saunders from Scarborough. These continual changes tell their own story. The company was unable to retain the actors for long and the constantly shifting membership must have told on the performances. It was a vicious circle.

During the Harrogate season Miss Sarah Booth was engaged for a few nights and her benefit was held on 8th September when she played Annette in *The Magpie or The Maid* and Little Pickle in *The Spoil'd Child*. It was announced as being her last night but on 12th September she appeared again as Amanthis in *The Child of Nature* and Priscilla Tomboy in *The Romp*. Beazley's *Is He Jealous?* was also given this evening. On both occasions box prices were raised to 4/-. Since February Mrs. Butler had been considering selling the circuit. In a letter dated 9th February 1818, the Rev. James Tate[105] made enquiries of G. W. Meadley:

> Two Gentlemen of Sunderland one of them I think a *Publican* in *Vine Street*, have been negotiating to take *Mrs. Butler's Circuit of Theatres* on apparently very fair terms. The scrap of paper on which their names were marked, I have mislaid. H. was the initial, to the best of my memory, of one or both of them. Are they *good* men & *true*? Your report shall be sacredly kept in any way that you desire. Yet to guard Mrs. Butler against harm concerns me just now not a little.

The report was evidently not favourable because on 16th March Tate wrote again:

> Let me thank you very kindly for the useful intelligence regarding Messrs. *Hodson & Holmes*. Mrs. *Butler* will now be sufficiently on her guard, without betraying any unhandsome suspicion. I have taken due care in any communication to avoid any hint or phrase; which even, if it should meet their eye, could create any reasonable offence.

In spite of this Holmes had joined the company in September and by October, when the company was at Richmond, Hodson and Holmes from the Theatres Royal Birmingham and Newcastle had taken over the company. A set of seven handbills has recently been discovered[104] which form an almost complete record of their season at Richmond from 5th October to 4th December 1818, including an interval for a visit to

Northallerton, 12th – 25th October and another, for some unspecified reason, 18th – 30th November. Four different printers were employed on the bills: Maclaren, Craggs, T. Bowman and Bell and their styles ranged from Gothic to classical. Because the theatre was closed for a longer time than was anticipated, a night was set aside for the benefit of the players among whom receipts were equally divided. Mr., Mrs. and Miss Butler still performed with the company along with George, Stoker, Young, Mr. and Mrs. Jefferson, Mr. and Mrs. Saunders, Mrs. Murray and Miss Stoker from the Butler regime. Newcomers were Bennett and Garthwaite from Newcastle, Mr. and Mrs. Andrews from the Haymarket, Mr. and Mrs. Tyrer from Glasgow, Fitzowen from Lincoln, Williams, Miss Hill, Miss C. Hill, Mrs. Melville and Miss Hodson (her first appearance on the stage). Vincent Decamp, who made a starring appearance on 6th and 9th November, was about to take over the Newcastle Theatre Royal. Shakespeare was represented by *King Lear*, (not acted here for many years) with Holmes as Lear, *Romeo and Juliet* and *The Merchant of Venice. A New Way to Pay Old Debts* and *The Rivals* were also revived and among new plays were Raymond's *Castle of Paluzzi* (G. G. 1818) and Soane's *Falls of Clyde* (D. L. 1817).

George Butler (now from the Haymarket) returned to play at Whitby from 14th – 23rd December. On 27th January the managers engaged Junius Brutus Booth from Covent Garden 'whose similarity and equality to Mr. Kean of Drury Lane is admitted, for a few nights.' During his performance nothing under full price was taken. As a rule half price was taken at 8 o'clock, the performances beginning at six, whilst children were admitted to boxes and pit at half price from the beginning. On 18th January Young performed Mortimer in *The Iron Chest* 'in which part he will take leave of his friends in Whitby, prior to his first appearance in that Character at the Theatre Royal, Hull.' The season lasted until 5th March when the playbill requested all tradesmen to send in their accounts. The company played four nights a week instead of three and their varied repertoire consisted of 15 comedies, 13 farces, 12 tragedies, 10 melodramas, 6 comic operas, 5 plays, 3 musical farces, 3 pantomimes, 1 burlesque, 1 ballad opera, 1 dramatic opera, 1 operatic romance, 1 interlude. For the first time Shakespeare headed the list with 9 plays (*Henry IV, Lear, Romeo and Juliet, Hamlet, Richard III, Othello, Cymbeline, Merchant of Venice,* and *As You Like It*); Colman the Younger followed with 8 and O'Keeffe with 4. Massinger's *New Way To Pay Old Debts*, advertised as the play which established Kean's reputation, was revived. A number of new plays were given; new to London in 1818 were Planché's *Amoroso*, Pocock's *Rob Roy McGregor*, Raymond's *Castle of Paluzzi*, R. Jones's *Green Man*, Shiel's *Bellamira;* new to London in 1817 were Soane's *Falls of Clyde* and Phillips's *Man in the Moon.*

Probably the season was not a success since henceforth Whitby drops out of the circuit. Only odd companies visited the theatre after this: i.e. the child prodigy, Clara Fisher in July 1821 and a company which included the Darleys in January 1828. The theatre was burned down on 25th July 1823 owing to the carelessness of some strollers who had engaged it for a few nights. The ruins were sold by the proprietors and George Young remarks that 'as for some years past it has been a losing concern, it is not very likely to be soon replaced.'[106] However there are playbills in the British Library for Whitby 1830-44.

The company's other winter station, Kendal, was lost too as a bill for 12th April 1819 announces that Howard's company from Lancaster had taken a lease of the theatre, which they continued to play in 1820, 1821, 1822.[109] Hodson and Holmes were evidently still in command when the company visited Harrogate on 4th June 1819 since the playbill states that:

> . . . The Managers most respectfully announce to the Nobility, Ladies and Gentlemen, at Harrogate and its Vicinity, that the Theatre will be Opened *in the Race Week only*, with three New Pieces never acted there.

No mention is made of Mrs. Butler. The three new pieces were *The Green Man, Amoroso* and *The Man in the Moon*. Samuel Butler played in the first two and Holmes took the part of the Green Man. Boxes were henceforward raised to 4/-. The players had returned to Harrogate by 17th June when they presented *The Farce Writer* for the first time there. The season continued until 2nd September which was announced as the last night of Kean's engagement. On this occasion the lower boxes were raised to 5/-, the upper boxes remaining at 4/- and an apology for this augmentation was expressed in the playbill:

> The Managers feel peculiar gratification in announcing to the Public, their success in having secured the Services of Mr. Kean, for Three Nights. In consideration of the difficulty of obtaining the above unrivalled Performer, at this period, the great request that he is in, and the high terms which the display of his talent commands, it is hoped a trifling advance of the Prices of Admission will not be objectionable.

Kean played Alexander in Lee's *Rival Queens* to the Roxana of Mrs. Hodson and the Statira of Miss Butler. Samuel Butler played Lysimachus. Kean then moved on with the company to Richmond where he played on 6th September Sir Edward Mortimer in Colman's *Iron Chest*.[108] Other parts were taken as follows: Fitzharding – Saunders, Wilfred – Butler, Adam Winterton – George, Samson – Hodson, Orson – Jefferson, Armstrong – Brown, Robber – Stoker, Boy – Miss L. Stoker, Helen – Miss Butler, Blanch – Miss Hodson, Barbara – Mrs. Saunders. Though, as we have seen, Kean had acted in his youth with the company this is the first time, as far as we know, that he had trodden the Richmond boards. The farce was *How To Die for Love* which was cast as follows: Baron – Brown, Capt. Blumenfield – Butler, Capt. Thalwick – Saunders, Trick – Jefferson, Trop – Hodson, Bricklayer – George, Charlotte – Miss Butler. A similar apology for the advanced prices graces this bill, the charges being boxes 4/-, pit 3/-, gallery 1/-. 'The three top seats of the pit, the price of the boxes.' This method of raising part of the pit into the boxes on special occasions was quite a usual one. Doors were opened at six and the performance began at seven. It is not known whether Kean gave any further performances in Richmond. Mr. Fisher, an ex-Town Clerk of Richmond wrote that 'Mr. Kean is known to have performed in the Theatre as L. Junius Brutus' but whether on this occasion or no is not discoverable. The company had taken the New Theatre in Thirsk and the last two nights of its performance there are recorded on playbills in the British Library. On 1st October they performed *She Stoops to Conquer* with Butler as Young Hardcastle, Miss Butler as Miss Hardcastle, Hodson as Tony Lumpkin, followed by two comic songs and *A Rowland for an Oliver*. On 2nd October, the last night, *A Cure for the Heartache* was given with *High Notions* in which Butler played the servant Bush; Miss Butler, Charlotte; Jefferson, the butler Timothy; and Mrs. Hodson, Martha a waiting woman.

By desire of the gentlemen of the Richmond School Colman the Younger's *Heir at Law* and Kenney's *Love, Law and Physic* were performed on 15th November.[109] The plays were cast as follows: *Heir at Law*: Daniel Dowlas – Saunders, Dick Dowlas – Butler, Dr. Pangloss – Wood, Henry Morland – Alexander, Stedfast – George, Zekiel Homespun – Hodson, John – Stoker, Kenrick – Jefferson, Deborah Dowlas – Mrs. Saunders, Caroline Dormer – Miss Butler, Cicely Homespun – Mrs. Wood. *Love, Law and Physic* Dr. Camphire – Saunders, Flexible – Forrester, Danvers – Alexander, Andrew – Hodson, John Brown – George, Waiter – Stoker, Lubin Loy – Jefferson, Mrs. Hilary – Mrs. Hodson, Laura – Mrs. Wood, Mary – Mrs. Saunders. In the interval Hodson recited *Soldier John's Return to Richmond*. Tickets were to be had of Mr. Bowman in the Market Place.

It will be noted that Holmes did not appear on either occasion and he had probably left the company. There had in a short time been considerable changes once more, and new names were Mr. and Mrs. Wood, Brown, Alexander and Forrester.

The company evidently stayed in Richmond during the winter and Mrs. Butler seems to have resumed her connection with, and possibly her control of it. But it was a melancholy state of affairs that the Rev. James Tate reported in a letter to his son dated 10th January 1820:[110]

The poor Theatre still opens to dismal emptiness. Mrs. Butler attempts a Benefit this Evening. But the continuance of severe weather makes charity doubly cold; when it has to show itself in a Play House.

The company's winter towns of Whitby and Kendal having been lost, they evidently stayed on late in Richmond. But the loss of these towns had disjointed the circuit and the company probably broke up for a while. Young Butler was acting with Manly's company in Nottingham in April 1820.[111]

Henceforward it seems probable that the company continued to disband during the winter and spring months, when Butler went as an actor to various other companies, and that it was brought together again for a summer and autumn season at Harrogate, Northallerton and Richmond. We have no evidence of a Harrogate season in 1820 but the company was acting in Northallerton in October of that year. One playbill advertises an otherwise unknown melodrama entitled *The Woodman and His Dog*, in which Butler played Count Rovezzo, a comic ballet called *Rival Lovers, or, All in a Bustle* in which Miss Butler danced Flora and the new farce *Too late for Dinner*. Another bill for 16th October announces the benefit of Holland and the last night of his engagement. He played Moses in *The School for Scandal* to the Sir Peter of Andrews, the Lady Teazle of Miss Butler and the Joseph Surface of Butler; in *The Dog of Montargis* which followed he played Blaize. There were several newcomers: Hamilton, Miller, Phillips, Richards, Mrs. Leonard, Miss Andrews, whilst Miss Craven reappears after an absence of three years. Who was managing the company we do not know. It was possibly Jefferson, who is mentioned as having a company of players in Bedale in a case that was brought against the actor Daniel Miller for theft, in December 1820. That Butler had played at Bedale is established in Hird's *Annals of Bedale* which mentions that the performances took place in a room and that they had full houses which brought in £20 a night. Bills were put up everywhere and the audiences came from all over, villagers servants and tradesmen mingling with gentry on bespeak occasions.[112]

The company was in Richmond by 7th November when Margaret Tate wrote: 'Last night my mother, aunt and I were at the Play it being the Mayors night – very poor amusement.' Richmond, it would seem, had lost its enthusiasm for the drama, and the company had lost its quality. This is confirmed by Christopher Clarkson who wrote in 1821: 'Theatrical amusements are very much upon the decline in this town.'[113]

By 1821 young Butler was definitely in command at the age of 18. The company was still good enough for Kean to pay a starring visit to them in Northallerton for a few nights. On this visit Donaldson has a pleasant, though possibly, apocryphal story to tell. (It seems to have been a Kean legend and was also related of his first starring visit to Taunton with Lee's company.)[114] The theatre being but small, prices for this occasion were doubled and the day after the first performance Butler waited upon Kean with £40, being half the receipts. Kean, however, handed back the money together with the account of cash taken at the door telling the astonished Butler to return it to his pocket. Kean then told the young manager the story of how the elder Samuel Butler had assisted him from that very town to accomplish his journey to London and had thus enabled him to start on his brilliant career there; so he was, he said, but paying to the son a debt for many years due to his father. Donaldson further tells us that Dibdin's pantomime of *Harlequin and Mother Goose* was then first performed at Northallerton with Kean as Harlequin and Butler as the Goose; thereafter the six foot tall Samuel was hooted after by boys in the street with the cry of 'goose – goose'.

Before the company reached Harrogate and was acting there in August and September Miss Butler had become Mrs. Piercy or Percy. Mrs. Renaud too had temporarily rejoined the company, this time with her husband. The only familiar names left are those of George, Jefferson, Master Jefferson and Barnett. Newcomers were Gordon, Swain, Macaulay, Bell, Mr. and Mrs. Mackay and Miss Russell. Macaulay played Jaffier, to Butler's Pierre and his sister's Belvidera in *Venice Preserv'd*, whilst *The Rivals* now had the following cast: Sir Anthony Absolute – George, Capt. Absolute – Renaud, Faulkland – Butler, Acres – Jefferson, O'Trigger – Mackay, Fag – Gordon, David – Swain, Mrs. Malaprop – Mrs. Mackay, Julia – Mrs. Piercy, Lucy – Miss Russell, Lydia Languish – Mrs. Renaud.

New plays were Walker's *Wallace* (with Butler as Wallace and Mrs. Piercy as Helen), an anonymous adaptation of *The Inconstant* called *Wine Does Wonders* (Renaud as Old Mirabel, Butler as Young Mirabel, Mrs. Renaud as Oriana and Mrs. Piercy as Bisarre), *The Promissory Note*, Price's *Quadrille* (Touchwood – Butler, Sophia Chainwell – Mrs. Renaud) and Poole's *Hole in the Wall*. The first three were produced in London in 1820, *Quadrille* in 1819 and *Hole in the Wall* in 1813.

In the autumn season at Richmond Macready appeared with the company, perhaps only for a night, on his way from Scotland. 'My "starring" course', he says 'pursuing its way through Carlisle, Richmond in Yorkshire, Scarborough and Whitby.'[115]

This year Butler spent the winter acting with de Camp's company at Newcastle and he remained there until May. Butler's movements in this and ensuing winter and spring months are not easy to follow as he has to be distinguished from George Butler. During the winter 1821-22, there was a Butler acting and stage-managing at Sheffield. That this was George, and that it was therefore Samuel who was at Newcastle, is evident from the fact that he is advertised as not having appeared there for six years. Samuel would then only have been 12, though he was acting in his mother's company.)[116] We may surmise that he then got together a company and visited Northallerton, though the first we actually know of him is in Harrogate in July. The company was almost entirely new.

On the opening night, 6th July, he promised the following ambitious programme of new pieces. Dibdin and Bunn's *Kenilworth*, Planché's *Vampire*, Dibdin's *Fall of Calais*, Waldron's *Miller's Maid*, Moncrieff's *Diamond Arrow*, *Spectre Bridegroom*, and *Monsieur Tonson*, Beaumont and Fletcher's *Wild Goose Chase*, Kemble's *Marmion*, Kenney's *Match Breaking*, Milman's *Fazio*, Poole's *Two Pages of Frederick the Great*, Keep's *Incog* and the otherwise unknown *Bachelor's Fare*. The growing popularity of the waltz, which had been scoffed at when introduced into England 20 years previously, is mirrored in the announcement that there would be a turn of waltzing by the Misses Smith from Liverpool. On 20th July Butler announced the engagement of Calvert from York, the same who had played with the company under the name of Young. He now starred as Virginius in the first performance at Harrogate of Sheridan Knowles's tragedy of that name. *Monsieur Tonson* was given its first performance there on 16th July by desire of the Hon. Mrs. Ramsay, announced as the 'Second Fashionable Night.' On 24th July *A New Way To Pay Old Debts* was followed by 'The Splendid Pageant of the Coronation of His Majesty George IV,' on which occasion no half price was taken. On 12th September Jefferson's farce *The Lady's Dream* was acted.[117] Harrington, Johnston, Wilkes, Mrs. Carey from Glasgow, Miss Anderson from Durham, the Misses Smith from Liverpool and Mrs. Hildreth (late Mrs. Fitzgerald) were all newcomers. Among the parts played by Butler were Col. Feignwell in *A Bold Stroke for a Wife*, Icilius in *Virginius* and Sir Giles Overreach. Primarily a tragedian, he evidently was at home also in the principal roles of comedy.

In Richmond on 22nd November Cumberland's *The Jew* and O'Keeffe's *Modern Antiques* under its sub-title *The Merry Mourners* were given as the school plays and the house fetched £24, six pounds less than it had done 13 years previously.[118] At the end of the Richmond season Butler rejoined de Camp at Newcastle where he stayed until May 1823.

A Harrogate playbill for 26th August 1823, announced that the theatre is to open for three nights only:

> ... and in order to give as great a Variety as possible to the Amusements of the Theatre, the Manager has engaged the following celebrated Performers; Signor Francisco and Signora Ferzi, (From the Gardens of Beaujon and Tivoli at Paris), and the surprising Monsieur St. Jean Parsloe, From Franconis at Paris. Whose performances were honoured with the presence of the Royal Family of France, on the 25th August, 1822, at a Grand Fete given by his Majesty Louis 18th.

Signora Ferzi was a juggler who concluded her feats by balancing a 'Chinese Pyramid Illuminated'; Signor Francisco performed the minuet and gavotte of Vestris on the tight rope and ended with a somersault display; whilst St. Jean Parsloe is described as the French Buffo who:

> . . . during his visit to London and Paris, completely astonished all beholders, and excited the surprise of the most eminent of the faculty, who conceived it impossible for the human body to display such pliability of limb as this phenomenon exhibits.

Their antics were the main business of the evening, *The Spoil'd Child* being thrown in at the end. The nights of performing are advertised as Tuesday, Thursday and Saturday but the company evidently prolonged their stay for another week, the next bill being for Thursday, 4th September for the benefit of Signor Francisco, the last night but one. On that occasion Signor Francisco, performed his 'wonderful Ascent on the Rope, From the back of the Stage to the back of the Gallery!!! Embracing the whole extent of the Theatre.' *Inkle and Yarico* and a bagatelle called *The Actress of All Work* in which Mrs. Piercy took six parts were also included in the programme. Butler's name does not appear but those of George and Master Jefferson do, together with the new names of Thompson, Comerford, Abbot and Mrs. Walker. On 25th August 1823 Frances Maria Butler petitioned the Mayor and Corporation of Richmond for a licence commencing on 30th September to be in force until November, the plays to be from the Westminster patent theatres and which had been submitted for inspection to the Lord Chamberlain (Museum).

The school plays at Richmond this year were given on 3rd November. *The Provoked Husband* and *Rungantino* were performed to a house which brought in £25. Butler again went to Newcastle for the winter and spring season. (A Butler was acting in de Camp's company in Beverley in June 1824 but as he was stage manager it was probably George. There is no evidence that Samuel ever held this position in de Camp's Newcastle company but George did in his Sheffield one.)

The following year, 1824, Samuel Butler came of age.[119] Again he started with an almost entirely new company. Only Brown, Mrs. Piercy, Mrs. Walker and Mrs. Carey remain from the previous year. Even old George and the Jeffersons have disappeared at last. David George died on 20th September 1831, at the age of 84 and is buried in Richmond Churchyard.[120] He was in harness until he was 76. The new players were Ford White, Huge, Hields, Burrows, Nelson, Wilton, Sefton, Sheridan, James, Angel, Mrs. Angel, Miss Walton and Miss M. Walton, child.

A few Harrogate bills are available for August and September.[121] New plays advertised were *Dolly and the Rat*, Croly's *Pride Shall Have A Fall*, Kenney's *John Buzzby*, Calcroft's *Bride of Lammermoor*, Bull's *Fortunes of*

Nigel, Howard Payne's *Clari* and *Charles II*, and Lunn's *Fish out of Water*. In *Clari* on 13th July Mrs. Butler made her re-appearance on the stage as Fidalma after an absence of seven years, that is, since the company passed to Hodson and Holmes. On 14th September Butler announced that he had engaged 'the celebrated Miss Lacey' from Covent Garden for three nights; this may have been Harriette Deborah Lacey, 1807-74 who received some training at Covent Garden before her debut in Bath, 1827.[122] In Harrogate she played Mrs. Haller in *The Stranger*. On 23rd September, the last night but two, a benefit for the prompter Wilton was given at which Sheil's *Adelaide*, 'justly considered the best production of the present day' was first performed in Harrogate. 25th September was the last night but one for the benefit of Mrs. Piercy. The company then went on to Richmond.[123] It must have reverted to Butler since the Museum possesses an application from him for a licence to play the statutory 60 nights, October to December, which is dated 9th September 1824. It is now definitely stated that a new company had been got together and that Butler was spending his winters as an actor under other managements.

> The playbill for the opening night on 5th October 1824 announces that: The Manager feels much pleasure in being able to introduce to the Public of Richmond his new Company, the talent of which has received the highest marks of approbation, and having the satisfaction of again appearing before them himself previous to his engagement at the Theatres Royal York and Hull.

The play was Howard Payne's comedy *Charles II* which had been produced at Covent Garden only five months previously. The cast was: King Charles – Butler, Rochester – Hields, Edward – Sheridan, Copp – Ford White, William – Brown, Gregory – James, Lady Claire – Mrs. Angel, Mary – Miss Walton, (from Newcastle). The afterpiece was E. P. Knight's farce *A Chip off the Old Block*: Sir Arthur Single – Ford White, Capt. Single – Hields, Farmer Lowland – Wilton, Robt. Lowland – Burrows, Andrew – Sheridan, Ellis – Clerk, William – Sefton, Chip – Angel, Lady Evergreen – Mrs. Carey, Emma – Mrs. Angel, Rose – Mrs. Walker, Jane – Miss. Walton. According to the critic of the *Sheffield Mercury* Butler's Charles II was inferior to many of his performances but yet had much talent about it.[124] The theatre was to be open every night during race week, tickets and places were to be taken at Bowman's and there was no half price. On 29th October at an evening under the patronage of the Mayor and Corporation *The Jealous Wife* was revived after an absence of seven years. The cast was: Oakley – Butler, Maj. Oakley – Ford White, Chas. Oakley – Ellis, Russet – Wilton, Ld. Trinket – Sheridan, Sir Harry Beagle – Angel, Capt. O'Cutter – Burrows, Tom – Sefton, John – Hields, Paris – Brown, Mrs. Oakley – Mrs. Piercy, Lady Freelove – Mrs. Angel, Maria – Mrs. Walker, Susan –

Miss Walton, Chambermaid – Mrs. Carey. The playbill announced that 'In the course of the evening a View of the Market-Place, painted by the late Mr. Cuit, will be exhibited.' The farce was *Modern Antiques*. On Monday, 8th November Timothy Hutton attended a play.

10th November was the last night but four for the benefit of Hields, Mrs. Carey, the Misses Walton and Sefton. Croly's *Pride Shall Have a Fall* was played in Richmond for the first time with the following cast: Ct. Ventoso – Ford White, Lorenzo – Hields, Col. Pistrucci – Sefton, Major O'Shannon – Ellis, Ct. Carmini – Sheridan, Torrento – Butler, Stefano – Wilton, Spado – Angel, Stiletto – Burrows, Lazaro – Brown, Pisonio – James, Countess Ventoso – Mrs. Carey, Victoria – Mrs. Angel, Leonora – Mrs. Walker. the farce was Lunn's *Fish Out of Water* which had been produced in London only the previous year; a revival of *Coriolanus* was promised before the season closed. *Coriolanus* had been played in Northallerton on 18th October when the company had broken their sojourn at Richmond, as was their wont, to play there during Race Week. The cast which was doubtless the same as that at Richmond was given as follows:[125] Coriolanus – Butler, Agrippa – Ford White, Cominius – Sheridan, Appius – Ellis, Y. Marcius – Miss. M. Walton, Sicinius – Wilton, Brutus – Burrows, 1st Citizen – Angel, 2nd Citizen – James, 3rd Citizen – Brown, Tullus Aufidius – Hields, Volusius – Sefton, Volumnia – Mrs. Angel, Virgilia – Mrs. Piercy, Valeria – Mrs. Walker, Servilia – Miss Walton.

Butler's Coriolanus was one of his finest roles and has been fully described by the critic of the *Sheffield Mercury:*[126]

Mr. Butler when clothed in the Roman costume, looked the hero he had to represent; he indeed seemed 'to bestride' the 'petty men' around him 'like a Colossus'. On his appearance in the first act, the mutinous citizens of Rome shrink into nothing at his approach, his look awes the discontented, and at his rebuke they melt away and disappear. Such a noble Roman as Mr. Butler's exterior presents, is alone sufficient to accomplish such a purpose - - - This nobleness of nature, this disdain to flatter even Jove himself for power, this propensity to wear his 'heart in his mouth', and the utter fearlessness of danger and death, for which Caius Marcius Coriolanus is distinguished, found an excellent representative in Mr. Butler. With the exception of a small portion of the second act, he was everything that could be wished. Occasionally, and only in a few passages, there was a want of energy when energy was required. In his subdued tones, the natural sweetness of his voice was sometimes lost in what, to our ears, nearly approximated to an unpleasant muttering, which was not always distinctly heard and understood.

Otherwise it 'was a masterly effort, a truly grand performance.' Particularly commended was the passage in Act III where he refuses Volumnia's wish that he should dissemble: 'I will not do't.' This 'was a fine outburst of genuine and noble feeling, moved almost to indignation at the base idea of so much degradation.' In the last act when his son is introduced, 'the manner in which he took him in his arms and pressed him to his heart was an exquisite touch of pure and tender pathos.' Lastly in the scene with Aufidius – 'Cut me to pieces Volsces' – he:

> . . . displayed all the excellencies and powers of his art – he was commanding and even terrific – one of the most masterly displays of passion and splendid execution that we remember to have seen.

On another occasion the critic said:

> We doubt if any man at present on the stage could perform this arduous character equally well with Mr. Butler: not one that we have seen, since John Kemble, can at all approach his excellence.[127]

On 19th October Fitzball's *Joan of Arc* was given in Northallerton for the first time. After the Richmond season had ended we may presume that the company broke up, and that Butler went to fulfil his engagement with the York company. (De Camp had given up Newcastle to Nicholson.) By March 1825 he was acting in York under Downe and Faulkner and is announced as being from Edinburgh. In the summer he again had a company for the season at Harrogate. On a playbill for 8th September 1825 Miss Moreton informs the people of that Spa that her benefit has been fixed for that night. The play was Kenney's *Sweethearts and Wives* which was followed by *Matrimony* and William Barrymore's melodrama *Meg Murnoch* which had been performed 70 successive nights at the Royal Coburg Theatre. A synopsis of the scenery and incidents of the melodrama was appended. Mrs. Butler appeared as Mrs. Bell in *Sweethearts and Wives*. Mrs. Piercy, White, Burrows and Sefton remained from the previous season, newcomers being McNamara, Ferrers, Walters, A. Turner, Frimbley, Mattison, Ivers, Mr. and Mrs. Clifton, Mr. and Mrs. J. Gann, Miss Shore and Miss Piercy. Butler's name does not appear on either of the bills.

Two Richmond bills are available for this year.[128] The first, which is dated 13th December 1825, announces the last night but one of Maria Foote's engagement.[129] She played Donna Violante in *The Wonder* supported by Butler as Don Felix, Young as Col. Briton, Potter as Don Pedro, Frimbley as Don Lopez, Grose as Frederick, Burrows as Lissando, White as Gibby, Turner as Algouzil, Wilson as Vasquez, Mrs. White as Isabella, Mrs. Grose as Flora and Mrs. Frimbley as Ines. In *The Weathercock* she played Variella in which she sang *Far, far from me my Lover flies* and the *Dancing Masquerade Song*. 'In consequence of the great additional expence attending Miss Foote's engagement' the prices were augmented to boxes 4/-, pit 2/6d, gallery 1/6d. No half price was taken and there was no admittance behind the scenes. The next night was her benefit and the last of her engagement. *As You Like It* was played with the following cast: Orlando – Butler, Duke Senior – Frimbley, Duke Frederick – Grose, Jaques – Young, Amiens – White, Le Beau – Brown, Oliver – Turner, Jaques de Bois – James, Sylvius – Wilson, Adam – Potter, William – White, Corin – Frimbley, Touchstone – Burrows, Rosalind – Miss Foote, Celia – Mrs. White, Phoebe – Mrs. Frimbley, Audrey – Mrs. Grose. As Rosalind Miss Foote sang the *Cuckoo* song and spoke the original epilogue. She then played Clara to Butler's Delaval in *Matrimony*. Butler seems to have acted in the company this year without managing it or being responsible for it, since the bill for 14th December announces that it is the last night but one of his engagement. On 25th December he appeared as Coriolanus in Sheffield, under the management of de Camp.[130]

By 19th June 1836 the two brothers, George Blythe and Samuel William Butler, were playing at Northallerton under the management of Samuel Wall Nicholson of the Newcastle company.[131] In July they both returned with him to Newcastle. It seems likely that this year Nicholson took over the Harrogate and Richmond seasons after he had finished his month in Newcastle. In L. T. Rede's *Road to the Stage*, printed in 1827, Nicholson is given as manager of Newcastle, Harrogate, Richmond and Northallerton. The salaries of the company are given as from one to one and a half guineas a week though larger salaries were paid at Newcastle. By December Nicholson's company was back in Newcastle with George Butler as stage manager and Samuel (sometimes put down as S. W. or W. S. Butler) as an actor. Here Donaldson met them both. S. W. Butler's name does not appear in the bills after 23rd May so that he evidently left about then with his summer company. He was in Harrogate on 28th August when a playbill announces that he had engaged John Pritt Harley from Drury Lane to play. On this night Harley played Dr. Pangloss in *The Heir at Law* in which character he sang the *Almanack Maker*; he also sang a popular parody on the *Bavarian Girls' Song*, written and arranged expressly for him by Parry, called *Buy A Mop* and then, as Somno in *The Sleep Walker*, he introduced imitations of Kemble, Munden, Bannister, Barrymore, Fawcett, de Camp, Blanchard, Betty and Matthews. For his second night on 30th August he played Acres in *The Rivals* whilst Butler had his old role of Faulkland, and then acted Barnaby Brilliant in Lunn's new farce *White Lies*, for a part which he had created a few months previously at Drury Lane. For his benefit on 1st September he played Mawworm in *The Hypocrite* and Lubin in *Love, Law and Physic*.

There is a Richmond playbill for the Grammar School play on Monday, 29th October the last night but one of the season.[132] The play was *Hamlet*

85

with the following cast: Hamlet – Butler, Claudius – Henderson, Polonius – Woodley, Horatio – Hardcastle, Laertes – Moss, Rosencrantz – Telbin, Guildernstern – Finlayson, 1st Gravedigger – Ford White, 2nd Gravedigger – Kitson, Lucianus – J. Waites, Ghost – Jefferson, Bernardo – Pierce, Marcellus – Kitson, Ophelia – Miss Cleaver, Queen Gertrude – Mrs. Henderson, Actress Queen – Mrs. Cleaver. Again the *Sheffield Mercury's* critic[133] has enabled us to have a glimpse of Butler in this role:

> Personal advantages for the part he is not richly stored with, being about three or four inches taller than any other Hamlet on the stage, but, he has intellect sufficient to compensate for all his other defects, even if they were more formidable than they are. Like Macready his acting is very unequal, sometimes rising to great excellence, and sometimes sinking even to mediocrity – His first speech ' 'tis not alone this inky cloak good mother' was very simply and beautifully given; and the soliloquy 'Oh that this too too solid flesh would melt' contained many exquisite touches of true pathos, and was finely delivered throughout; his interview with the Ghost was likewise well sustained.

In the scene with the gravediggers, he:

> . . . displayed great judgment and skill in his profession. His acting was quiet and unobtrusive, but natural and forcible in every part.

At another performance[134] the critic specially commended his first act:

> His speaking was mellifluous as the tones of the flute, and, occasionally, as soft, as tender, as melancholy, and as musical as the breathings of the Eolian harp.

The scene with the ghost reached sublimity. He was very successful too in his scenes in Act II with Rosencrantz and Guildenstern, the players and Polonius. His:

> 'I have of late (but wherefore I know not) lost all my mirth', was certainly never heard surpassed, not even by John Kemble, who always made a point of speaking this speech in his finest manner.

The Ophelia of Miss Cleaver was merely 'a respectable representation.'

Hamlet was followed by Richard Jones's farce *Too Late for Dinner*, cast as follows: Frank Poppleton – Moss, Frederick Poppleton – Henderson, Nicholas Twill – Jefferson, Pincroft – Ford White, Robert Rafter – Woodley, Mons. Fasnet – Hardcastle, Snip – Kitson, Gardener – Telbin, Watchman – Finlayson, Mrs. Thompson – Mrs. Cleaver, Miss Emma Somerton – Miss Cleaver, Miss Eliz. Pincroft – Miss Telbin, Letty – Miss Shore. A Jefferson had returned to the company but whether this was George or one of his sons there is no means of knowing. Only Ford White, Miss Shore and Butler himself remained over from the company of 1825, all the rest were new and had been recruited from far and wide. The Cleavers, Moss and Miss Macallan were from Newcastle, Henderson from Bristol,

Woodley and Miss Telbin from Scarborough and Hardcastle from Birmingham.

The company then went to Sheffield which had been vacated by de Camp and was now taken over by Butler who, as we have seen, had acted there under de Camp in 1825-6. The company remained largely the same as it had been at Richmond. It was said to be weak, Butler being the main attraction.[135] He was pronounced:

> . . . a very sensible man, as well as a powerful actor: he has a vigorous conception of his author's meaning, and he generally depicts the character he personates in a natural and forcible manner. He frequently rises to great excellence and never or but rarely approaches mediocrity in feeling, thinking or acting.

'One of the most promising young men in his profession,' 'a gentleman in conduct and manners, and in private life a worthy and amiable man' are other tributes. Yet with a poor company he often played to thin houses and the *Sheffield Theatrical Examiner* tried to drive him out of the town because he had employed one Johnson, of whom they did not approve, to repaint the theatre. The company opened on 5th November 1827 and remained at any rate until February 1828.

In the autumn of 1830 Samuel Phelps was again with Mrs. Butler's company in Sheffield.[136] On this or some other previous occasion at Sheffield he was left stranded and took the theatre from Mrs. Butler for one night's benefit.[137] Mrs. Butler then evidently was still the lessee of the Sheffield theatre when her son acted there.

Some time in the first half of 1828 Butler took into partnership one Cliff, a Sheffield bookseller.

On 31st July on a Harrogate playbill Messrs. Butler and Cliff 'respectfully announce that they have entered into an engagement with the Celebrated Mr. Kean Jun. for Two Nights Only.' Charles Kean appeared as Young Norval in *Douglas* to the Glenalvon of Butler, the Lord Randolph of Ellis, the Lady Randolph of Miss Cleaver and the Anna of Miss Telbin. This was followed for the first time in this theatre by R. B. Peake's little comedy *£100 Note*.

This year the School play at Richmond was performed on Friday, 26th September and was *Macbeth* with the original choruses by Matthew Locke.[138] The cast was: Duncan – Telbin, Malcolm – Miss Telbin, Donalbain – Jones, Macbeth – Butler, Banquo – Henderson, Physician – Brown, Macduff – Ellis, Rosse – Hill, Fleance – Miss E. Telbin, Seyton – Collier, 1st Officer – Nelson, 2nd Officer – Emden, Lady Macbeth – Miss Cleaver, Gentlewoman – Miss Nelson, Hecate – Jefferson, 1st Witch – Bland, 2nd Witch – Mrs. Cleaver, 3rd Witch – Miss Shore.

Butler's Macbeth does not seem to have been so outstanding as his Hamlet or Coriolanus. The *Sheffield Mercury* critic[139] says he 'must at present be content to take a station somewhat lower than Kean and Macready.' After the murder:

> . . . he displayed great skill and judgment. He has, however, one defect, which he should be reminded of – He is too much in the habit of emphasising monosyllables. If there is a pronoun in his way he sometimes lifts it into consequence 'he knows not why and cares not wherefore'.

The critic then repeats the charge that he sometimes sank his voice to an unintelligible growl or murmur and goes on to mention a third defect:

> . . . that he scarcely pays sufficient attention to the management of his person – his deportment is not always imposing and dignified. Sitting or standing, his figure occasionally presents too many angular lines.

Macbeth was followed by *The Critic* with: Puff – Butler, Dangle – Henderson, Sneer – Ellis, Sir Fretful Plagiary – Telbin, Mrs. Dangle – Miss Shore, Don Whiskerandos – Jefferson, Ld. Burleigh – Collier, Governor of Tilbury Fort – Nelson, Earl of Leicester – Emden, Sir Walter Raleigh – Hall, Sir C. Hatton – Brown, Master of the Horse – J. Telbin, Beefeater – Bland, Sentinels – J. Waites, Brown, Tilburnia – Miss Cleaver, Confidant – Mrs. Cleaver, 1st Niece – Miss Telbin, 2nd Niece – Mrs. Nelson. 'The Piece will conclude with the National Air of *God Save the King* by the Whole Company.' Tickets and places for the boxes were to be taken of Bowman and the theatre would be open on Saturday evening.

The company had been kept together through the winter and spring seasons at Sheffield and the services of Henderson, Nelson, Jefferson, the Telbins, the Cleavers and Miss Shore had thus been retained.

On 27th October Messrs. Butler and Cliff opened again at Sheffield with substantially the same company as had been acting at Richmond, but with some additions which included Mrs. Piercy.[140] They remained until 30th January but after that we do not know what happened to them. It was not they but another company altogether which visited Harrogate in 1829. A playbill for 30th July includes Hodson, Miss Craven and Darley, who had all been in the Richmond company at one time or another, but all the other names, the Greens, the Blandfords, the Robberds, Warren and Myers are quite new. The Butler connection with Harrogate was broken. This new company performed there an otherwise unknown:

> New Melo-Dramatic Pantomime (never acted here) interspersed with Marches, Dances and Broad Sword Combats called The Savage of the Desert, or African Gratitude.

The popular shipwreck of melodrama was included in the effects. The afterpiece was Bickerstaffe's *The Hypocrite*. Doors opened at 7, the performance commenced at 7.30 and second price was available at 9. This is the last we hear of the theatre at Harrogate. Grainge[141] says 'The company was broken up, the Theatre and decorations sold, and the building was converted into a lodging-house'; elsewhere he informs us that the company became bankrupt.[142] The theatre had been converted into dwelling houses by 1833.[143]

Which company it was, Butler's from Sheffield or this new one from Harrogate, which visited Richmond that autumn we cannot tell. Whoever they were they did not meet with success. George Croft wrote to his cousin James Peacock from Richmond on 1st November 1829:[144]

We have had your great Actor, Kean, performing at our Theatre – also Master Burke, but unfortunately for them, theatricals seem to be at a low ebb here, neither the superior talent of the one, nor the novelty of the other could half fill the small house at the usual prices, so that they could not profit much. We also had Miss Smithson, but I think little of her.[145] Madame Vestris was expected but does not come.

Timothy Hutton records in his diary on Tuesday, 27th October 'Went to the Theatre in the evening to see Kean perform. Was much pleased with him.' Master Burke was a well known child actor and musician. Wemyss thought little of him as the former but a good deal of him as a violinist.[146] Since even the great Kean could not draw an audience, what hope was there for a local company? Butler's lease of the Richmond Theatre expired in May 1830 and in December of that year the Corporation received a letter from Mrs. Butler 'desiring to become tenant of the Theatre in place of her son.'[147] For some reason this request was not complied with. A pathetic ending to Mrs. Butler's story is to be found in the minutes of the Lennox Lodge of Freemasons on 7th June 1849:

Mrs. Butler, Comedian, having made application to the Lodge for Assistance, being in adverse circumstances, the sum of 10s. was unanimously voted out of the funds for her relief.[148]

Though the Richmond stage was to see Samuel Butler no more, a few words remain to be said about his subsequent career and his reputation as an actor. Butler, this year without Cliff, ran his third and last season of management at the Sheffield Theatre in the winter of 1829-30. From March to May 1830, he had a company in York which included Samuel Phelps, Jefferson, Mrs. Piercy, Angel and Miss Angel.[149] The season was unsuccessful, and later in the year, according to Wallett,[150] Butler was managing a summer theatre in Hull. He, together with Mrs. Piercy and Jefferson, was with W. J. Hammond's York company in 1831[151] but by December he and his wife, of whom we hear for the first time, were in America acting at the Bowery Theatre, where he did not prove a success. He played Coriolanus, Virginius and Sir Edward Mortimer and is described as from the Edinburgh and Bath Theatres. (I have been unable to trace him at Bath.) He soon returned to the English provinces, but we next hear of him playing at Covent Garden as Hamlet, and on 6th November 1832, as Stefano Diamante in *The Dark Diamond* 'with great spirit.'[152] He is now described as from the Dublin company. He subsequently acted at the Surrey and other minor theatres and in 1839 succeeded Charles Matthews as manager of the Olympic.[153] On 28th and 29th October he played *Hamlet* and *The Avenger* at Brighton. He failed, but undeterred, opened in June 1842 at Tivoli Gardens, Richmond Hill, U.S.A. with Butler's Vaudevilles and Promenades only to meet further failures. His wife, however, appeared with considerable success.[154] He returned to England in August 1843. Ireland says of him as Hamlet that 'handsome in person, graceful in action and correct in elocution, he still lacked the inspiration necessary to rank him as an artist of the first class.'[155] But the fullest description of his powers as an actor comes from Westland Marston who saw him play as a star at the Surrey.[156] He was thoroughly in earnest, well trained in his art and of a commanding presence:

> The extreme height of Mr. Butler, indeed, was a disadvantage to him in a small theatre. – he was a good elocutionist, and – he had the excellent quality of abandoning himself to passion without self-criticism – being already a proficient in the technical resources of his art, he trusted himself in good faith to the leading impulses of the character. I do not think he was given to rant. He occasionally exploded in sudden, vehement bursts, but they had the effect of being spontaneous – the outcome of passion accumulated and repressed. In the crisis of feeling you saw, in him, that passion though sometimes intensely in white heat, dart forth at others in fiery tongues and roars – I do not care to use a weaker phrase – in its ascent. He was gifted, moreover, with a powerful voice, and had no need to hide the defects of a feeble physique by feigning that mysterious self control which has since been called 'repressed force.' – In Shylock I was more carried away by him, so genuine was his passion, than by any other actor I have seen in the part. I will not undertake to say that his interpretations were as profound as they were undoubtedly vivid. I do know, however, that he was 'terribly in earnest' and that he had the power of rousing masses to enthusiasm. His excessive height as has been said, was a great disadvantage, and stood in the way of his being fully appreciated.

His height also impressed John Coleman[157] who met him in Robertson's company in Leicester and describes him as:

> . . . a remarkable and portentous–looking person of middle age, who stood some six feet or more in his shoes.

He later adds that:

> . . . through the instability of his temper and his hauteur and severity of manner, he failed to make friends. Everyone feared, no one loved him.

He opened as Hamlet in Leicester:

> . . . and a very ponderous but powerful and scholarly performance it
> was. He omitted (after the John Kemble fashion) all the early part of
> the famous soliloquy which ends Act II, and commenced with
>
>
>
> I have heard
> That guilty creatures sitting at play . . .
>
>
>
> When he came to the lines, 'The play's the thing,' etc. he rushed to the
> table, snatched up a pen, and with 'eyes in a fine frenzy rolling' began
> coram populo, to write the lines 'with which to catch the conscience of
> the king'

a bit of business which Robertson disapproved of but other actors copied
and were praised for. Coleman continues that:

> Butler's performance of King John, The Stranger, William Tell,
> Shylock, Robert Tyke, and Richelieu, to my immature mind appeared
> to be of the highest order of excellence, and I have since heard the same
> opinion expressed by persons far better qualified to form an opinion.

He found Richelieu his most impressive impersonation and the best save
Macready's; his least impressive Don Caesar 'a truly funereal effort'.
Coleman sums up:

> Although he failed to attain the highest honours of his craft, he was an
> actor of distinguished ability. That he was a scholar and a gentleman
> there could be no doubt.

Some portraits of him are fittingly extant in the 1d plain and 2d coloured
juvenile theatre prints where he appears as Caractacus and as Walder in *The
Avenger*; there is also a vignette of him as Hamlet published by T. Heath.[158]

After Butler returned from America and when Coleman met him, he
was suffering from 'a terrible internal malady.' This compelled him to give
up the stage and resort to Shakespeare readings and lectures. He was
engaged for a series at the Athenaeum, Manchester, previous to his
intended final retirement. He opened on 16th July 1845 with *The Merchant
of Venice* but was taken ill and had to be conveyed home. The following
evening whilst walking in his chamber, he fell dead in the arms of his wife –
this version from *The Era*.[159] According to the *Gentleman's Magazine*[160] he
dropped dead on 21st July on his way home from the reading. Coleman says
he died after a performance as Pierre at the Pavilion Theatre. The
Gentleman's Magazine gives his age as 40 but he must have been 42 or 43.
His funeral was attended by a large circle of stage folks in the
neighbourhood. He is buried in Ardwick Cemetery. As a result of his long
illness he left his widow in embarrassed circumstances but Manchester,
where he had been a favourite, gave her a benefit which, Donaldson tells us,
was never exceeded even 'in that mart of commerce.'

CHAPTER V

The Subsequent History of Richmond Theatre 1830 – 1984

AFTER THE BUTLER COMPANY had ceased to exist, Richmond Theatre was from time to time taken for a season by various managers. But the old circuit was forever finished and these odd visits were irregular and makeshift. For some years the theatre does not seem to have been occupied at all though on 25th August 1832 the committee of the Corporation recommended that the theatre should, if possible, be let and not remain unprofitable to the Corporation.[161] That same year Northallerton Theatre was closed and was subsequently taken over by the Primitive Methodists for their services.[162]

Perhaps a company played for a few days in Richmond during Race Week in 1835 for an entry under the rental income of the Corporation for that year reads: 'Cash for the use of the Theatre £1.0.0d.' But the first definite knowledge we have of the theatre's being used for its proper purpose after the collapse of the Butler regime is in a letter from George Croft dated during Race Week 18th October 1837.[163] He writes:

Our Theatre is open at present and we have a most respectable Company. Young Meadows played for four nights here. The audiences were very poor considering that he was rather famous and Richmond his native town.

This must have been Drinkwater Meadows whom we last heard of in 1815. The reception which the company engaging him met with was evidently not encouraging. Yet on 30th March of the next year, 1838, the Coucher Books record a motion that the theatre be let for the ensuing fortnight to Mr. Jones for two guineas; an amendment resolved that the rent be £2.10.0. (There had been a Mr. Jones in Butler's company in 1828.) A playbill of Jones's season is to be found at the Bishop Blaize Hotel. The date is 4th April 1838 and the performance was for the benefit of Mr. and Mrs. Hodgson:

. . . who respectfully solicit the inhabitants' patronage on that

92

occasion, hoping that the entertainment selected for their amusement will be such as will ensure them that portion of public support it will ever be their study to deserve.

Tobin's *The Honeymoon* was the main offering and was thus commended in the bill:

This Comedy is one of the finest pieces of Comic Acting that the stage has produced, the Language is exquisitely finished: it has all the beauty and freshness of the Golden Age of Poetry; and the sentiments throughout are pleasing, dignified and natural; and the author by one happy effort of Taste and Genius attained a rank in Literature to which the vapid and multifarious productions of his contemporaries shall in vain aspire.

The cast was: Duke of Aranza – Young, Count of Montalban – Smith, Balthazar – Booth, Lampedo – Brierly, Campillo – Elton, Pedro – T. Jones, Lopez – D. Jones, Jaquez – Findlay, Juliana – Mrs. T. Jones, Volante – Mrs. Booth, Hostess – Hodgson. This was followed by the much admired Nautical Drama *The Sea – The Sea, The Open Sea Or the Haps and Hazards of the Ocean Child:* (Produced at the Royal Pavilion, Whitechapel Rd. in 1834). In this Capt. Mandeville – Booth, Capt. Sturdy – Smith, Harry Helm – Findlay, Dennis O'Trott – Young, Koherk and Giles Clump – D. Jones, Snowball – Wells, Jack Junk – Fountain, Neptune – Smith, Peter Poultice – T. Jones, Capt. Worthyman – Elton, Lieut. Manly – Hodgson, Old Curious – Brierly, Amphitrite – Mrs. Hodgson, Attendants – Mrs. Booth, etc., Mary Helm and Margery O'Trott – Mrs. T. Jones. The synopsis of this melodrama will give an idea of the type of fare it was:

Cabin of Windsor Castle – Attempts of Capt. Mandeville on Mary Helm who is protected by her husband – a designing scheme to rid the vessel of Harry Helm. Apparent friendship of the Captain. Deck of the Windsor Castle – A Sailor's Scene – Preparations for christening the Ocean Child – Appearance of Neptune and Amphitrite who christen the child – Grand Nautical Chorus, the Sea, the Sea, the Open Sea – Harry Helm is dispatched to the Grosvenor – Cabin of the Grosvenor – Arrival of Harry who delivers his message but is detained. His resolute determination to return to his wife – His desperate resistance and exit through the cabin window into the sea. The seamen throw out a rope. And Harry Helm is brought exhausted on board. – Consternation of the Captain at the discovery of his seamen, the latter are triumphant – Harry Helm is condemned to walk the plank – He attempts to get on board, when his hand is severed from his body – He falls into the sea exhausted – A Storm at sea – Part of the wreck of the Windsor Castle discovered – The bowsprit extending sufficiently to realise the two beautiful pictures of Daive, first a beautiful female struggling with an infant in her arms against the raging billows, second that of a brave seaman letting himself down from the bowsprit, and thus suspended between air and ocean snatching the mother and her infant from a watery grave. The piece terminates with the death of the Assassin – Happiness of the Ocean Child and apothesis of Harry Helm.

The prices of seats had fallen since Butler's day, the boxes were 2/-, pit 1/-, gallery 6d and children as before went half price to the pit and boxes. The doors opened at 6.30, the play commenced an hour later and half price was available at nine to boxes and pit. Tickets were to be had at the Fleece Inn, Mr. John Harker's, Mr. Doughty's, Oak Tree Inn, and Mr. Hodgson's.

On 9th August the Committee on houses was authorised 'to make such repairs to the Theatre as are absolutely necessary'; and the Coucher Books record orders for the paying out of the borough fund of £1.0.9d. to Richard Horner for slates and carriage for the theatre on 9th September; of £2.3.2d. to Messrs. Norman and Metcalfe for repairs on 14th November; and £1.14.6d. to William Gill for wood used in repairs on 25th January 1839. Meanwhile on 31st August the Mayor was requested to inform a Mr. Colling of Hunslet that the Council had agreed to treat with him for a 21 years' lease and to arrange a meeting with him. Evidently these negotiations came to nothing, as we hear no more of them.

The repairs had been put in hand for Burton's company and a good part of the expense was paid by him. He gave an autumn season for which two playbills are extant in the possession of Mr. T. Eyles of Richmond. The first announces a performance on Saturday, 29th September under the patronage of the Richmond Agricultural Association. Benjamin Webster's melodrama *The Golden Farmer* was presented with the following cast: Golden Farmer – Mercer, Old Mob – Montague, Jemmy Twitcher – Burton, Peter Piebald – Crowther, Paul Piebald – C. James, William Herbert – Wilson, Bowl – Smith, Porter – Master Burton, Thomas – Charles, Elizabeth – Mrs. Burton, Louise – Mrs. Wilson. (The bill is partly torn off so that the exponents of Harry Ham and Betty are missing.) The blurb reads:

the story of the Golden Farmer has a two-fold object; it shows that vice may be reclaimed by the — and example of virtue; that the felon may become a useful member of society by the all-powerful influence of those kindly affections that twine around the heart; it further shows, that when the desire of heaping up riches has taken possession of the mind virtuous resolutions, the deepest resolutions, the deepest contrition, proves but weak barriers against any temptation, etc. etc.

The second bill for 26th October for Sheridan Knowles's *William Tell*: . . . under the patronage of the President, Vice-President and Gentlemen members of the Richmond Harmonic Society; on which occasion the Concert Band of the above Institution have kindly offered their services, and in the course of the evening, will play several favourite Overtures, etc.

The performance was for the benefit of the Mercers and family, who duly solicited 'for auld lang syne' the patronage of the ladies and gentlemen of Richmond. These then must have been the Mercers who were for so long attached to Butler's company. The cast was: William Tell – Florrington, Albert – Miss H. Mercer, Verner – Mercer, Gesler – Montague, Erni – Burton, Meletel – Crowther, Sarnem – C. James, Emma – Miss Mercer. Between this and the afterpiece the *Keel Row* was sung by Mercer and the Misses Mercer, Harriet and C. Mercer. The afterpiece was M. G. Lewis's melodramatic romance *One O'Clock or the Knight and the Wood Demon* with Count Hardyknute – Montague, Guelpho – Crowther, Willikind – Burton, Rolf – C. James, Osway – Smith, Leolyn – Miss H. Mercer, Sangrida – Mercer, Una – Miss Mercer, Spirit of Alexina – Mrs. Coppin, Clothilda – Mrs. Burton, Paulina – Mrs. Montague, Auriol the fairy – Miss C. Mercer. Prices had reverted to boxes 3/-, pit 2/-, gallery 1/- with half price at 8.30 and children under 12 at half price at the commencement. Tickets were to be had of Mercer, or of T. & A. Bowman where places for the boxes could be taken.

Burton planned to be a regular visitor for on 7th February 1839 an application from Thorn of Ripon to take the theatre was refused on account of:

> Mr. Burton who had the Theatre during the last Autumn having expended several pounds in fitting up the Theatre and expressed his desire to take it again.

A bill for his spring season dated 9th May 1839 hangs in the Bishop Blaize Hotel. A new nautical melodrama *The Wrecker's Daughter* was performed (this is not Sheridan Knowles's melodrama of the same name) with Cann – Florrington, Col. Travers – Thompson, Frederick – B. Tannett, Will Bobstay – Burton, Simon Swipes – Brunton, The Stranger – Willmore, 1st Wrecker – Adams, 2nd Wrecker – Swann, Mary – Miss Atkinson, Julia – Miss Villiers. The programme of scenery and incidents is worth quoting in full:

> Act 1st. Scene 1st. Interior of the Dolphin Public House on the coast of Cornwall. Bobstay among the Breakers. Grog for twelve and six to drink it. A Sailor's description of his sweetheart. Thunder. A Gun fired. Signals of distress. Alarm and consternation. Who is the man in the mask?
>
> Scene 2. Extensive view of the ocean. In this scene will be exhibited a new grand and *Moving Sea. The Wreck.* Another lurch – She founders. 'Tis music to the Wreckers, 'Tis his harvest hymn.

A lapse of 12 months is supposed to occur between 1st and 2nd Acts.

> Act 2 and Scene 1. Interior of the first. Simon Swipes, a candidate for the temperance Society. A Sailor's Wedding. A Pas Seul. Not in the

least admired by Bob who prefers dancing a Sailors Hornpipe. The Festivities are interrupted by the arrest of Captain Frederick Dervan for a murder committed 12 months since. Tableau.

Act 3 and Scene 1. Let the proud beware how he wounds the feelings of his inferior fellowmen. Trifle not with the heart's bitterness. Impunity has its limits. A flint will fire when you strike it. A Sailor's method of consoling a Broken Heart.

There's a sweet little cherub that sits up aloft
to keep watch for the life of poor Jack.

Scene 2. Meeting between Cann the Wrecker and Colonel Travers. The Wrecker, the only evidence against Captain Dervan, swears to the sword found upon the Captain as the one belonging to the murdered Stranger twelve months since. Twenty years has the Wrecker brooded vengeance, but now 'tis within his grasp! A Sailor's method of making a Staircase. Give him a coil of rope or a hank of spun yarn and he'll make you a fine pair of stairs as you will see in a day's cruise.

Scene 3. Exterior of the Eagle's Tower. Heroic conduct of Cann's daughter. She charges her father with the most dreadful crime, and vows to give him up to justice if he does not assist in the escape of Dr. Dervan. Interior of the Eagle's Tower. A mysterious Adventure. One Arm is seen protruding through a Trap Door. Bob seizes it and discovers the long-looked for Larboard Finn. The Murderer discovered. Grand Tableaux.

All very absurd it sounds but I doubt if a synopsis of some of our present day films would sound any less so. The afterpiece was Kenny and Millingen's farce *The Illustrious Stranger* with King Aboulifar – Thompson, Prince Azan – B. Tannett, Gimbo – Brunton, Alabajon – Adams, Princess Arza – Miss Villiers, Fatima – Miss Atkinson. The Mercers had evidently left Burton's company.

The state of the Theatre came under consideration by the Council in December 1839. On 6th December they resolved not to enter into contract with Mr. Hooper for it, and on 10th December they sat to determine upon the best mode of converting or disposing of it as a source of profit to the borough fund and of advantage to the public. They came to the conclusion that the best use that could be made of it was to convert it into a Borough Court. They proposed to carry a good floor over the pit, to level up the stage so that it could be used for sales, exhibitions, institute meetings, and the like by which revenue might accrue to the borough fund. As for the part under the stage, then forming the dressing rooms, together with the ground floor composing the pit, these would be offered for lease as warehouses or vaults; the boxes and gallery to be left as they were, as they would be useful appendages to a court of justice or place of public audience. The Committee was to agree on a plan and specifications for effecting the flooring, to ascertain the expense and report. A month later on 10th January the Primitive Methodists approached the Council with a view to renting for seven years 'the upper part excluding only so much of the stage as is separated from the Audience by a curtain,' provided that the Corporation did certain alterations. This offer was declined because the Council had appropriated part of the building for another purpose. On 8th September the committee on houses was required to carry into effect the recommendation of the finance committee with regard to the theatre, the expense to be defrayed by the borough fund. Whether this recommendation was the same as that of 10th December or another we do not know. The order had not been carried into effect by 10th January for on the 4th of that month 1841 it was resolved to let the theatre once again to Burton for five weeks from the following Wednesday for £5, the rent to be paid to the treasurer before Burton was allowed possession.

The order of the finance committee was to be carried out after the expiry of Burton's occupation. An amendment proposing that Burton's application be refused and the theatre be appropriated for other purposes forthwith was defeated. Another amendment throws a vivid light on the life of the theatre; it proposed:

That the Gallery of the Theatre under several former managements having been a Source of great disorder and immorality from being the resort of bad characters who have deterred respectable persons from visiting it, and also has been a great annoyance to the Audience who have occasionally attended the other parts of the House, that this should be closed, the entrance effectually barred, and the pit divided into two prices if, thought desirable.

This amendment was rejected by the Mayor's casting vote.

Burton duly opened his season for which we have two playbills at the Bishop Blaize Hotel. The first of these announces the great success and last night of Master Owen from all the principal theatres in the Kingdom on 17th February 1841.[164] He played Douglas with the following cast: Old Norval – Banks, Lord Randolph – Lomas, Officer – George, Lady Randolph – Burton, Glenalvon – Lewis, Donald, First Officer – Nilson, 2nd Officer – Thompson, Anna – Mrs. Brown. This was followed by the anonymous melodrama *Red Rivan; or The Bandit's Bride;* Red Rivan – Banks, Lord Vandeman – Lomas, Jermuck – George, Ulric – Lewis, Malcoff – Burton, Murven – Thomas, Durwin – Smith, Oliska – Mrs. Smith. No orders or free admission were available during Master Owen's engagement, but the usual half price was obtainable at 8.45. The bill promised performances every evening during the week. Master Owen's 'triumphant success' was extended: on 19th February the last night but one

97

of his engagement was announced. On this occasion he had the temerity to essay Hamlet, the other parts being taken as follows: King – Banks, Laertes – Lewis, Polonius – Burton, Ghost – Brown, Rosencrantz – Thomas, Osric – George, Guildenstern – Lomas, Gravedigger – Burton, Gertrude – Mrs. Burton, Ophelia – Mrs. Banks. This was succeeded by Egerton Wilks's farce *State Secrets* with Hugh Nevile – George, Calverton Hal – Lewis, Hedgehog – Thomson, Robert – Lomas, Gregory – Burton, Letty – Mrs. Banks, Maud – Mrs. Burton. Master Owen was announced as Macbeth for 21st February 'Being for his Benefit and positively his last appearance in this Theatre.'

That some alterations to the theatre were effected that summer is proved by an entry in the Coucher Books under 11th June ordering a payment of £10 from the borough fund to the Chamberlain on account of alterations and improvements. But that this did not include the laying of a floor over the pit seems evident from the fact that the theatre again housed players in October, though this time not Burton's. A playbill in possession of Mr. W. Wilson of Richmond for Tuesday, 12th October 1841 announces that:

> . . . there will be brought forward the new Melodramic adaptation (in three parts) from the very celebrated Novel called Jack Sheppard, adapted by J. T. Haines.

Jack Sheppard was cast as follows: Sir Rowland Trenchard – Rickatson, Mr. Kneebo – Healey, Owen Wood – Mellison, Jonathan Wild – Elgin, Thomas Darrell – Smith, Blueskin and Abraham Mendez – Thomson, Warren, John Dumps – Cook, Jack Sheppard – Liver, Lady Trafford – Mrs. Liver, Winifred Wood – Mrs. Rickatson, Edgeworth Bess – Mrs. Rickatson, Mrs. Wood – Mrs. Elgin, Mrs. Sheppard – Mrs. Liver. The bill is mutilated so that only the final scenes can be quoted:

> Four strongholds in Newgate – his wonderful Escape – the dying Mother and her son – Jack's distraction and vow of revenge – Willesden Church Yard – the Mother's Grave. JACK IS TAKEN. Procession to the Place of Execution – takes an affectionate farewell of his Pals – The Gallows – Wild's Triumph – JACK IS unbound by Blueskin who gives him a pistol – Jonathan seeing this fires – Jack falls – Wild's house in Flames – and The Thief taken by the mob is HURLED INTO THE BURNING RUINS.

The afterpiece was J. B. Buckstone's farce *Mischief Making:* Henry Degrais – Rickatson, Oliver Guiot – Smith, Nicholas Dovetail – Liver, Villager – Moore, Madame Manette – Mrs. Liver, Jacquette – Mrs. Elgin, Louise – Mrs. Cooke, Jane – Mrs. Warren, Therese – Mrs. Rickatson. Boxes were reduced to 2/6d, pit 1/6d, gallery 6d and half price at 9 meant that boxes were 1/6d, pit 1/- and there was no reduction for the gallery. Monday, Tuesday, Thursday and Friday were performing nights.

This is the last playbill of performances at Richmond, though others, doubtless, took place, Mr. Foster ex-Town Clerk, mentioned a performance of Kenney's *Blind Boy* with Blanchard's *Pork Chops* and the same author's *Artful Dodge* which he assigned to 1840; but it must have taken place at earliest in 1843 since *Pork Chops* was not brought out at the Olympic until 13th February of that year and the *Artful Dodge* dates from February 1842. Lord Russell, who was born in 1834, recalls that the theatre was seldom occupied in his childhood but from what he remembers of the bills, the pieces were of the bloodcurdling order.[165] His account of the theatre is somewhat fanciful. The bills were taken round to each house door.

> I can see as if it were yesterday the person who brought our bills. He was a tallish man of saturnine aspect, with a shaven, swarthy face, long, oily, dark hair, and some pretensions in his shambling manner. It was positively stated, and was thenadays deemed credible, that this sallow, shabby-genteel bill circulator was himself the leading actor of the troupe.

He adds that Charles Kean and his wife (Ellen Tree) acted at Richmond within living memory. This may refer to Kean's visit in 1828, but if it means after his marriage which took place in 1842, it must apply to a much later one. On 15th November 1841 payments of £1.2.10d. to John Harland for mason's work on the theatre, and of £2.0.0d. to the Chamberlain on account of expenses in altering the theatre were ordered to be paid from the borough fund. On 5th June 1845 we read that the theatre's conversion into a public room for the use of benefit societies and other purposes had been deferred for want of funds. In October 1846 it was leased to one Martha Loftus for a month for £3 but whether for theatrical entertainments does not transpire. On 4th January 1847 the application of John Frankland of Sunderland to rent the theatre was refused as he had not produced sureties. It was then agreed to hold a special meeting to arrange for the proper lighting and altering of the theatre in order to make it useful and profitable as a public room.

Its doom as a playhouse was finally sealed in 1848 when the lower part was rented for 10 years to Croft as a wine vault and the upper part for a three year term to Miller as an auction and general room. Yet a further application for its use as a theatre was made in a letter from one Teasdale and Herr Johann Rossoff, dated from Sheffield, 12th June 1852, who inquired whether it was at liberty that season, the terms on which it was available and its size. In 1855 it was occupied by the militia so that the quadrille party which had hitherto been held there sought accommodation at the Town Hall. Alderman Croft's lease of the cellarage was extended for another 10 years but Jacob Hills, who evidently was in possession of the upper portion and was not occupying it, was given notice to quit on the following May

99

Day. This upper portion was then let to Alderman Croft on the same terms as the lower. A renewal was granted to J. G. and C. G. Croft in 1871 for 21 years.

After serving as a cornchandler's, furniture depository and, at the beginning of the war, as a salvage depot, it was finally restored to its use as a theatre on Monday, 2nd August 1943 in commemoration of the 850th anniversary of the enfranchisement of the Borough. The work was hastily completed, in spite of wartime obstacles and restrictions, in the space of a month and plays in a curtain setting were given once a week. Once more a playbill was printed and a prologue by Sagittarius broke 'the silence of a Hundred Years.' The Richmond Players presented Act II of J. B. Fagan's *And So To Bed*, to which was added Eden Phillpotts's *The Purple Bedroom* presented by those successors of the theatre's old patrons, the gentlemen of the Grammar School. These two pieces and Helen Jerome's *Charlotte Corday*, presented by the Richmond High School Old Girls' Association were given during the week turn and turn about. After this the theatre was once more dismantled and it was not until 1960 that the Georgian Theatre Trust was established owing to the initiative of Lady Crathorne and David Brooks, the Town Clerk, who launched a successful appeal to reinstate the theatre. Dr. Richard Southern was called in to make a thorough investigation which led to the theatre's complete restoration as an 18th century playhouse. The reopening took place in May 1963. Since then many occasional productions have been staged. In 1978 a Theatre Museum was opened in a warehouse, adjacent to the playhouse,[166] thanks to the initiative of Mr. Gregor MacGregor. In four rooms are displayed playbills and memorabilia of the theatre which include Edmund Kean's snuff box. One room is devoted to the reopening in 1963 and another houses a mock-up of the stage on which is displayed a set of scenes of 1836 from the studio of George Rivers Higgins of Royston, some of the earliest scenery in England.

Appendix

List of Plays Otherwise Unknown

The following plays, performed in Richmond or by Butler's company in the circuit, are not mentioned in the *Biographia Dramatica*, Nicoll's *18th Century Drama* and *19th Century Drama*, or Clarence's *Stage Cyclopaedia* and, as far as I am aware, there are no other traces of them. They are listed in order of their appearance.

Whitby Lasses or A New Way to Get Rid of a Wife.
Entertainment
Whitby, 14th February 1794.

Beverley Lasses.
Beverley, 26th May 1794.

Les Ombres Impalpables or The Whimsical School of Proteus.
Harlequinade.
Whitby, 13th January 1795.

The Good Son.
Farce.
Low School, Richmond, 21st November 1799.

Coal Trade or Adventures in a Coal Pit.
By Stephen Kemble.
Whitby, 14th February 1806.

Reformation or What We All Want.
Comic Drama by Mrs. Felix.
Whitby, 8th February 1808.

Black Forest or Robbers of the Cave.
Serious Pantomime.
Whitby, 28th February 1813.

Harlequin Sundial or Time's a Tell Tale.
Harrogate, 17th September 1814 (2nd Time).
Whitby, 11th March 1816.
Ripon, 16th April 1816.

Indians or the Punishment of Treachery.
Serious Pantomime.
Whitby, 5th February 1816.

The Miser or The Mysterious Purse of Gold.
Pantomime.
Whitby, 6th April 1816.

Woodman and His Dog.
Melodrama.
Northallerton, 13th October 1820.

Bachelor's Fare.
Promised at Harrogate, 1822.

Dolly and the Rat.
Farce.
Harrogate, 5th August 1824.

Savage of the Desert or African Gratitude
Melodramatic Pantomime.
Harrogate, 30th July 1829.

The Wrecker's Daughter★ or the Larboard Finn.
Nautical Drama.
Richmond, 9th May 1839.

★ This is a different play from Sheridan Knowles's *The Wrecker's Daughter*.

Notes

Chapter 1

1. The Tate papers were shown me by the late Miss Warman. They are now in possession of Mr. L. P. Wenham. Blomefield *History of Norfolk*, 1808, Vol. VIII, gives John Tayleur, rector of Aldeburgh, 1730, Suffield 1738, Gunters and Hanworth 1757

2. Ms. shown me by the late Miss Warman

3. *Ibid*

4. *Memoirs of the Life of Mrs. Sumbel, late Wells*, 1811, I,32. 1776 was the year in which she acted with the York company

5. For actors mentioned in the Richmond Parish Registers, see L. P. Wenham 'Richmond Parish Registers, 1771-1842 References to the Players of Richmond'. *Richmond and District Civic Society Annual Report*, 1978, 23-5

6. *The Wandering Patentee*, 1795, II, 154

7. *Thespian Dictionary*, 1805

8. In possession of Mrs. Butler of Milnthorpe

9. Cornelius Nicholson, *Annals of Kendal*, 1832, 123. A previous theatre connected with the Football Inn, Market Place, had been opened by Thomas Ashburner in 1758

10. Brit. Lib. provincial playbill collection

11. Elizabeth, born in 1777, was only a child. This is her only known appearance on the stage as she did not become an actress

12. He was with the York company during the whole of 1786. Tate Wilkinson, *op. cit.* III, 23

13. Tate Wilkinson first visited Harrogate in 1774, *op. cit.* II, 36

14. *Ibid*. II, 37

15. Inserted in Corporation Coucher Book

16. Thomas Sheppard, *The Evolution of the Drama in Hull*, 1927, 52

17. Tate Wilkinson, *Memoirs*, 1790, IV, 51-6

18. George Oliver, *The History and Antiquities of Beverley*, 1829, 280

19. The diary is in possession of Air Chief Marshall Sir Christopher Courtney who kindly allowed me to quote the relevant passages. I have been greatly helped in the interpretation and copying by Miss I. M. Bromley, a great great grandchild of the diarist. John Courtney was born in 1734, the only child of John Courtney who by marriage had come into a good deal of property round Beverley. The diarist was an M.A. and LL.B of Trinity College, Cambridge, a J.P. and Deputy Lieutenant for the East Riding. He married Mary, daughter of William Smelt of the Leases, Richmond, and died at the beginning of 1806 (information from Miss Bromley)

20. William Grainge, *A Guide to Harrogate*, 1861, 22; *The New Harrogate Guide*, 16

21. This and other Harrogate playbills mentioned are in my possession or in the British Library

22. *Thespian Dictionary*

23. *D.N.B. cf. Clarkson Stanfield*, Tyne and Wear Museums Exhibition Catalogue, 1979.

24. *Notes & Queues* 8th Series. XI, 301-2

Chapter 2

58. Christopher Clarkson, *The History of Richmond*, 1821, 207
25. Christopher Clarkson, *The History of Richmond*, 1821, 207
26. Bryan, *Dictionary of Painters and Engravers*
27. Richmond Burial Registers, No. 11
28. The Museum, Beverley; kindly copied for me by Mr. J. Dennett, F.S.A., Town Clerk of Beverley
29. *Authentic Memoirs of the Green Room*, [1806] 209
30. *The Reminiscences of Thomas Dibdin*, 1827, I, 107
31. J. Genest, *Some Account of the English Stage*, 1832
32. James Boaden, *Life of Mrs. Jordan*, 1831, 165
33. Mrs. Cornwell Baron-Wilson, *Memoirs of Harriot, Duchess of St. Albans*, 1839, I, 52. Charles E. Pearce, *The Jolly Duchess*, p. 31. points out that, if 1777 be accepted as the date of her birth, she was only 11 at this period
34. Baron-Wilson, 84; *D.N.B.*
35. T. Wilkinson, *Wandering Patentee*, III, 106
36. *York Chronicle*, 25th June; playbills in Brit. Lib.
37. *York Chronicle*, 17th Sept.
38. *Times*, 7th August 1943; letter from Miss Bromley
39. J. F. Curwen, *Kirkbe Kendall*, 1900, 319
40. 2nd Nov. 1790; *Theatre Notebook*, I, 78
41. Probably refers to Richmond, Surrey, *D.N.B.* under George Davies Harley
42. Guildhall Library playbill
43. *York Chronicle*, 16th Aug.
44. Farrar, *History of Ripon* 2nd ed. 1806; *Ripon Millenary Record*, 1886, 114. Information from Miss Hobson
45. George Young, *A History of Whitby*, 1817, II, 636
46. W. Donaldson, *Recollections of an Actor*, 1865, 167
47. Brit. Lib.
48. March 1797
49. William Winter, *The Jeffersons*, 1881, 1; *Monthly Mirror*, 1804
50. Guildhall playbill, 18th July
51. Wakeman's House, Market Place, Ripon
52. Produced Drury Lane, 14th Dec. 1797. Already given by the company in Whitby
53. Brit. Lib. playbills
54. Sept. 1800
55. *York Chronicle*, 27th Sept. 1800
56. 2nd ed. 1813, 102
57. 1885, p. lxiv

Chapter 3

58. C. W. Bardsley, L. R. Ayre, *Registers of Ulverston Parish Church*, 1886, 625
59. *Ibid*, 520, 523. C. W. Bardsley, *Chronicles of the Town and Church of Ulverston*, 1885, 8
60. Presumably the building in Daltongate which Mr. A. W. Holmes informed me is now used as a hayloft. The previous theatre was a barn attached to the White Horse Inn.
61. Holcroft's *Deaf and Dumb* was brought out at Drury Lane, 24th Feb. 1800; Allingham's *Fortune's Frolick* at Covent Garden, 25th May 1799
62. Reynolds's *Life* was brought out at Covent Garden, 1st Nov. 1800; Fawcett's *Obi* at the Haymarket, 2nd July 1800
63. Wemyss, *Theatrical Biography*, 1848, says that Miss Butler was about 17 in 1817
64. *York Herald*, 8th August

65. Information from Mr. E. Bush
66. William Watkins, *The Fall of Carthage*, Whitby, 1802
67. It was Race Week with which the Beverley season was timed to coincide
68. Probably *The Magic Oak or Harlequin Woodcutter* produced at Covent Garden in 1799, but in a Kendal playbill of 1807 it has the sub-title of *Harlequin Triumphant*. Allingham's *Marriage Promise* was brought out at Drury Lane, 5th March 1803
69. Colman's *John Bull* was brought out at Covent Garden, 5th March 1803
70. In the Rev. Tate's Diary under 13th Jan. 1820 is a small note 'Samuel Butler will be 21 in 1824. This for the property in Harrogate'
71. T. Meadows, *Thespian Gleanings*, 1805
72. Barrow-in-Furness Library, Soulby Collection of playbills
73. I have seen only the 2nd edition, 1813
74. Brit. Lib.
75. Courtney Diary, 18th May 1805
76. Oliver, *op. cit.*
77. Geo. Poulson, *Beverlac*, 1829, 447
78. Winter, *op. cit.*
79. Donaldson, *op. cit.* says 1805, but the date 1806 given by F. W. Hawkins, *Life of Edmund Kean*, 1869, I, 59 must be correct for Proctor, *Life of Edmund Kean*, 1835, I, 52 says that he acted with Rae during his first season at the Haymarket and Rae did not appear there until 1806
80. Donaldson, *op. cit.* this seems more likely than Phippen's story that he was 'applauded very much in the characters of Hamlet, Lord Hastings and Cato', *Authentic Memoirs of Edmund Kean*, 1814
81. Playbills in Columbia University, Brander Matthews Dramatic Museum
82. T. Moore, *Letters and Journals of Lord Byron*, 1833, I, 101
83. Soulby playbills
83a. Playbill, Birmingham Public Library, Shakespeare Vol. 2
84. Columbia University
85. Soulby playbills
86. Richmond Corporation Coucher Books
87. Diary in possession of Lady Curzon-Howe; references kindly supplied by Mr. Bush
88. Robert Dyer, *Nine Years of an Actor's Life*, 1833, 232
89. *Ibid*, 236
90. According to a tablet in the church; *York Chronicle*, 18th June 1812, gives the date as 8th June; the Parish Register, kindly examined for me by the Rev. T. H. Tardew, merely gives June. His tomb in St. Mary's Church says 15th June, aged 62
91. Thos. Sheppard, *op. cit.*

Chapter 4
92. In possession of Mrs. Carter, Northallerton
93. Sheppard, *op. cit.*
94. *Theatrical Biography*, 1848, 35
95. Richmond Burial Registers, 1813-35, No. 11
96. Coucher Book
97. Huddersfield, 1823
98. *D.N.B.*
99. *Op. cit.*

100. *D.N.B.*
101. I owe information on this season to the files of the *Westmorland Advertiser* which they kindly allowed me to examine at their Kendal office
102. Possession of Richmond Theatre Museum
103. George Young, *A History of Whitby*, 1817, II, 636
104. For these see L. P. Wenham, 'Theatre Royal, Richmond 1818', *Richmond and District Civic Society Annual Report*, 1980
105. Possession of Mr. L. P. Wenham
106. *A Picture of Whitby*, 1824, 251
107. Brit. Lib. playbills
108. Playbill, formerly in possession of Messrs. Fraquet, King Street, Richmond; present whereabouts unknown
109. Playbill in possession of the Grammar School
110. Possession of Mr. L. P. Wenham
111. Brit. Lib. playbill. Donaldson, *op. cit.* met him there
112. L. P. Wenham, 'Notes on the Georgian Theatre, Richmond', *Richmond and District Civic Society Annual Report*, 1979, 19-20. Also published by the North Yorkshire Record Office
113. Clarkson, *History of Richmond*, 207
114. Dyer, *op. cit.*
115. Macready, *Reminiscences*, ed. Sir Frederick Pollock, 1875, 232
116. For Newcastle and Sheffield seasons see Brit. Lib. playbills and *Sheffield Mercury*
117. Printed in Jefferson's *Theatrical Eccentricities*
118. Tate's Diary
119. *Ibid*
120. Burial Register No. 11
121. Brit. Lib. and in my possession
122. *D.N.B.*
123. Three playbills Brit. Lib.
124. 15th Dec. 1827
125. Playbill Brit. Lib.
126. 8th Dec. 1827
127. 31st Jan. 1829
128. Brit. Lib.
129. Afterwards Countess of Harrington, *D.N.B.*
130. Also Jaques on 7th Jan. and Joseph Surface 8th Jan. Playbills Brit. Lib.
131. Brit. Lib. playbills
132. Possession of the Grammar School
133. 17th Nov. 1827
134. 3rd Jan. 1829
135. For detailed criticisms of the company's performances see *Sheffield Mercury*, 1827-9
136. W. May Phelps and John Forbes Robertson, *Life of Samuel Phelps*, 1886, 36
137. John Coleman, *Fifty Years of An Actor's Life*, 1904, I, 154
138. Grammar School playbill
139. 22nd Dec. 1827
140. *Sheffield Local Register*, Nov. 29, 1829

141. Grainge, *A Guide to Harrogate*, 1861, 22
142. Grainge, *History and Topography of Harrogate*, 1871, 107
143. *The New Harrogate Guide*, 1833, 88
144. Information from Mr. Bush
145. Harriet Smithson, 1800-54, later wife of Berlioz. *D.N.B.*
146. W. Clarke Russell, *Representative Actors*, 386n
147. Coucher Book
148. Information from Mr. Bush
149. Brit. Lib. playbill; *York Chronicle*, 18th March, 29th April 1830; *York Herald*, 22nd May 1830
150. *The Public Life of W. F. Wallett*, 1870, 2
151. Brit. Lib. playbill
152. Brit. Lib. Covent Garden cuttings 1789-1834
153. Erroll Sherson, *London's Lost Theatres*, 1925
154. C. D. Odell, *Annals of the New York Stage*, 1928, III, 569; IV, 537, 598
155. Joseph Ireland, *Records of the New York Stage*, 1867, II, 368
156. *Our Recent Actors*, 1888, I, 26
157. *Players and Playwrights I Have Known*, 1888, II, 142; *Fifty Years of an Actor's Life*, I, 153-7
158. L. A. Hall, *Catalogue of Dramatic Portraits in the Theatre Collection of Harvard College Library*, 1930, I
159. 27th July 1845
160. Aug. 1845
161. Coucher Book
162. J. L. Saywell, *History and Annals of Northallerton*, 1800, 143
163. Information from Mr. Bush
164. George Owen the original Oliver in the dramatisation of *Oliver Twist*, 1838; also appeared at Birmingham and Newcastle that year and was about 14 when he acted at Richmond. H. Oswald, *Theatres Royal in Newcastle upon Tyne*, 1936, 95; M. T. Odell, *More About the Old Theatre, Worthing*, 1935, 134
165. *Thenadays*, c. 1904
166. Penelope Zetland, 'The Georgian Theatre Richmond' *Richmond and District Civic Society Annual Report*, 1978, 28-9

INDEX

108

110

111

112